THE POLITICS OF CRITICAL THEORY

Language/Discourse/Society

George Snedeker

University Press of America,® Inc.
Dallas · Lanham · Boulder · New York · Oxford

55673214

2-1-05

Copyright © 2004 by
University Press of America,® Inc.
4501 Forbes Boulevard
Suite 200
Lanham, Maryland 20706
UPA Acquisitions Department (301) 459-3366

PO Box 317
Oxford
OX2 9RU, UK

Library of Congress Control Number: 2003116380
ISBN 0-7618-2815-X (paperback : alk. ppr.)

For Danielle

CONTENTS

Michael E. Brown

Northeastern University

In these essays, Professor George Snedeker re-engages the question, "what is critical about critical theory?" The problem is initially posed in regard to Perry Anderson's rejection of "western Marxism" as a framework for the formulation of politically relevant theory because of what he sees as its essentially subjectivist tendency (Anderson, 1976). Professor Snedeker's response tacitly acknowledges that evaluating any theoretical tradition for its present relevance requires taking into account the sociological, and therefore political, significance of the imposition of the desocializing universalization of exchange now most often referred to as "globalization." The over-riding metatheoretical question which is raised and addressed in various ways in this book is how the authors discussed by Professor Snedeker conceive of the relation of theory to practice *if Anderson's negative characterization of the tradition of "western Marxism" is unacceptable as stated and if their conceptions are to be understood as capable of responding to the effects of globalization.*

It is possible to think of criticism generally enough to include Lukacs, the Frankfurt School, and Habermas, as well as Marx according to a widely shared conception discussed at some length by Raymond Geuss. According to this, there are three important characteristics of critical theories which distinguish them from positive theories: their intention, their form of argumentation, and the conditions of their validation (cf. Geuss, 1981, pp. 55-56). On this account, their intention is to contribute to the liberation of humanity. But liberation requires enlightenment, which, in its negative form, involves bringing to notice the coerced or manipulated aspects of what otherwise stands for self-knowledge in society.

The standard example is the critique of ideology in which propositions held up as worthy of belief (e.g., "those who work are rewarded according to what they accomplish," "capitalism is a necessary condition of democracy") are shown to involve presuppositions about human affairs and their arrangements which cannot be made explicit without unsettling those very propositions (e.g., if democracy is a function of society, the proposition "capitalism is necessary for democracy" begs the question of how the private economy allows for the reproduction of the social aspect of productive labor, hence of society). From this point of view, the critique of ideology begins with the question "what further proposition(s) would provide sufficient reason(s) to believe the proposition(s) in question?" It evaluates these further propositions according to their internal consistency, their compatibility with the idea they purport to make explicit, what they must exclude in order to provide a logical basis for the propositions in question, and their compatibility with what other ideas and beliefs about human affairs cannot be rejected as things stand. Ideology critique attempts, among other things, to demonstrate one or more of the following points. First, certain propositions, brought to notice by the politics of an intrinsically oppositional social relation, are predicated on more primitive propositions which are not true or are otherwise unacceptable. Second, such propositions are predicated on the possibility of universal application where the conditions of demonstrating that possibility require a redefinition of the universe (e.g., society) in such a way that only some of those who must be included are in fact included (e.g., given that capitalism is inconceivable without the production of commodities by the application of labor power, "everyone can be a capitalist" implies that "'everyone' excludes at least some laborers"). Finally, such propositions depend on omitting what is essential to their possibly being true (e.g., the idea of "cost of production" cannot acknowledge the necessity of "concrete labor" to production).

Propositions which fail these and other tests, and are therefore incomplete where they claim to be complete, irrational when they appeal to rationality, and/or based on what cannot be true as things stand, are, for this sort of critique, properly called "ideological propositions." The hegemony of an ideology lies largely in the ways in which its discursive practices deny the legitimacy of the act of criticism itself. Apart from this, for the critique of ideology to succeed in contributing to liberation and enlightenment, the critical demonstration must show itself to be non-ideological in at least one sense. It must display sufficient evidence of self-reflection that its success includes prospects of further criticism and self-criticism (as, in effect, a self-justifying and inherently liberatory project). This is in contrast with ideology which aims to put self-reflection and discussion, therefore politics, and for that matter society as such, to an end.

It follows that the distinctive form of argumentation of critical theories is reflective, in contrast with the objectifying intention of positive science. This is not to say that there is no room for positive science in a critical theoretical account of society, but that instrumental reason operates within and is conditional upon there being some self-critical and socially reflexive process of determining what is and what is not a proper object of manipulation and control. To say that critical argumentation is reflective without limits (and therefore self-reflective) is to agree that knowledge of human affairs is always contextual and theory is "itself always a part of the object-domain which it describes." Thus the reflective character of critical theory has to do with the critical fact that such "theories are always in part about themselves," and this is a necessary condition of the validity of positive concepts of human affairs prior to their submission, if appropriate, to empirical test and evaluation (Geuss, 1981, p. 55; for an altogether different sense of the idea of "critique" see Robert Nozick's off-hand dismissal of critical theory as little more than the rejection of ideas before better ones are available, in Nozick, 1981, p. 631n).

It is in this light that it is reasonable to make the following distinction: the validation of strictly positive theories has to do essentially with their fit to a shared reality, while critical theories are acceptable only to the extent to which they reveal a basis of criticism as immanent to (or an internal feature of) their object. The classic example is Marx's demonstration that the concept of the capitalist mode of production (the object of his critique) is valid to the extent to which it refers to something which is, on its own part, essentially self-critical, namely the contradictory relation of the social production of commodities to the universalization of exchange. In that sense, his critique of "capital" finds itself within its object (as conceived) and the object and the theory are thereby shown to be historical (and critical) through and through.

Given the three characteristic features of critical theories, it is possible to see the history of sociology in the United States from the 1950s until the end of the century as attempting to draw a fine line between positive and critical conceptions of its quality as a science of human affairs — where only the rationality of the positive conception had been clarified as a general foundation for the attainment of knowledge. In that case, the history of sociology can be summarized roughly in terms of two totalizing oppositions. One consists of an opposition between the residual effects of "structural functionalism" (and therefore the idea of the "social system") and the attempt to demonstrate the validity of two critical ideas. The other has to do with the incompatibility of the idea of society with its technical realization as a concept.

The first of the two ideas which appear to subvert the concept of a social system is that its theory elided its own necessary condition, namely ceaseless mobilization, what Derrida once referred to more abstractly as "the play of structure." The second is that the theory was most easily read as an attempt to distinguish between what was and what was not socially rational, and to do so on the grounds of a pretheoretical, or received, distinction between "institutional" action and the socially constitutive activity of people in motion which falls outside of the institutional order. In other words, the idea of a social system was not compatible with the socially inclusive idea of action on which it depended for its justification as a theory of society (cf. Brown, 1986).

The denigration of popular social movements implied by the functionalist theory was held up to critical scrutiny precisely at a time when such movements were particularly momentous, toward the end of the 1960s. The politics of that period led many students of "collective behavior" to rethink the implication that the ends and means of social movements (and crowds) fall outside of "the conditions of rational action" (cf. Brown and Goldin, 1973). Since this rethinking came in the wake of an enormous body of literature critical of the American political economy in particular regard to issues of equality, justice, and democracy, the attribution of rationality to "collective behavior" was tantamount to affirming a sense that institutional rationality could no longer be taken for granted. It had, instead, to be radically qualified by reference to socially irrational factors such as power, ideology, class antagonisms, and the maldistribution of wealth. Functionalism, with its assumptions that the unity of society is essentially institutional and that the institutional order constitutes virtually exhaustive conditions of rational action, could scarcely withstand the conceptual assault which accompanied the political and ideological struggles of the 1960s and beyond.

However, no alternative general theory was available in the main stream literature of sociology nor was one immediately forthcoming in the light of events. What substituted for theory were the pragmatics of the struggles for equality, justice, democracy, and recognition. The increasing complexity of the referents of these struggles, and a growing acknowledgement of the fact that they were more intelligible as international or global movements than strictly national ones, produced a lexical and conceptual field for rethinking the role of popular movements, popular culture, and even revolutions in the on-going constitution of democratic society. This, in turn, provoked considerable rethinking of the very concept of democracy. The idea that the term refers only to activity within the institutional structure of the capitalist state began to give way to more socially progressive ideas of participation and a greater degree of trust in the capacity of popular mobilizations to provide a socially reflexive rationality more relevant to democracy than the outcome-oriented rationality posited by functionalists as all the rationality there could be (cf. David Bogen, 1999). Democracy was, then, only conceivable as a process and not a system in the functionalist sense of the term; in which case the same had to be said of "society" itself. Thus, objections to structural functionalism as well as the effect of events on the theoretical imagination led to a remarkable new discourse on the social and political dimensions of human affairs and to an appreciation of the rationality of social movements which, as a matter of logic, cast doubt on whether or not the rationality of institutional action could any longer be taken for granted.

The second opposition remained in the background of the attempt to shift the focus of social change from elites to society (conceived of on other than system grounds); yet it shadowed each turn in the discussion, primarily because there was no clearly articulated theoretical alternative to structural-functionalism within the main stream of sociology. The most important re-emergent figure in this was Marx, though a Marx whose work had been variously interpreted throughout the twentieth century precisely in regard to the tension between the notion of society, which was necessarily a critical notion, and its technical sociological concept as non-critical and essentially positive. Specifically, the debate represented a tension between Marxism, interpreted positively as political economy in, for example, Paul Sweezy's influential study of Marx's *Capital,* (1942*),* and the more generalized notion of critique derived from the tradition Perry Anderson (1976) referred to as "western Marxism" and identified initially and largely with the Frankfurt School, and later with the work of Jürgen Habermas and a literature which came to be referred to as "post-structuralism."

On the side of criticism, there was general agreement about the values to which theory had to be oriented if it was to have social validity (and therefore to stand for shareable knowledge). These included justice, equality, the priority of people over profits, and, therefore, economic as well as political democracy. However, there were other, fairly serious disagreements. For one, the positive interpretation of Marx's critique of capital as political economy, essentially radical economics, suggested either too limited or too extensive a role of capital in the life of society. Either the capitalist mode of production was a parallel development to society and therefore the latter had its own dynamics, or it was identical with (or the fundamental cause of) the development of society as such.

In the first case, political economy provided knowledge that could be made publicly available, effectively correcting misapprehensions about the operations of capital and the rationality of capitalists. Rational political action, from this point of view, essentially involves teaching, in the sense of disclosing what is otherwise hidden; and it involves doing so in such a way that the critical disclosure corresponds to a prior though not necessarily articulate intuition on the part of those who share the situation it purports to clarify. This version of Marxist thought has done its job in at least one respect. It has provided, and continues to provide, information and a frame of reference for criticizing economics (especially in regard to the relation of price to value and to the conditions of inequality) which none of the social sciences and humanities can now ignore. But it tended to leave out of its most rigorous formulations the life of society and the possible rationality of those a different age referred to as "the masses."

On the other hand, the idea of capitalist production, as not only a framework within which societal events work themselves out but an effective force which in one way or another (e.g., structurally or causally) determines the most important directions of social change (independent of the sheer fact of power), seemed to exclude any notion of a self-determining popular politics and, indeed, to omit what Marx identified as at least two sources of relative autonomy in the development of culture and society, namely what he referred to as the bearers of labor power and the social determination of the wage. It also seemed incapable of explaining resistance and opposition other than as pure reflections of economic facts, and of accounting for the possibility of Marxian theory itself. The latter point reinforced the view that Marx's critique did not amount to an exemplary instance of critical theory and thus could not illuminate capitalist society as an historical, self-critical totality. This accounts, in part, for the continued skepticism about "western Marxism" as insufficiently theoretical and insufficiently materialist, though not in regard to the claim that it overemphasized subjectivity. The intuition that there was something to the criticism of positive tendencies in Marxism supported continued interest in the relationship between agency and culture/society. In this sense, subjectivity remained a shadowy presence in most attempts, especially those responsive to Gramsci, to realize the connection of Marxist theory to any form of politics but a strictly institutional and efficiently rational form.

There were two types of response to the apparent split between the subjective and objective aspects of Marx's work. One tended to treat his critique, the early works of Lukacs, and Frankfurt School sociology as providing insights while relying on severely reduced simplifications of what might otherwise have been read as systematic attempts to formulate a viable theory of society or, say in the case of Marx, a viable theory of certain limitations on society imposed by the capitalist mode of production. This emphasis on insights (in contrast with systematic theory) had important consequences for reformulating the problem of mobilization which made functionalism seem untenable in the first place. One was a tendency to focus on the capacity of social movements themselves to produce the theories they needed in going beyond the mere facts of congregating or sharing an interest or condition to the politically crucial facts of social formation and relative power. In regard to this, recourse to insights from the canonical figures of "western Marxism" did not derive from a desire to elevate the notion of subjectivity to a position above political economy so much as from the desire to formulate the possibility of politically viable agency in the midst of capitalist modernism and not solely at the moment of its "last instance." For this one could find provocative and useful comments in *Capital* and *History and Class Consciousness* and, for that matter, *Dialectic of Enlightenment,* without having to engage in the debates over the theories themselves.

Second, there was a tendency, partly in opposition to the critical dimension of critical theory, to see Marxism as an attempt to clarify a pragmatic idea of modern inequality derived essentially from the unjust distribution of wealth. This tendency was mainly identified with Eric Olin Wright's version of "analytic Marxism" (cf. Wright, 1989). It drew at least some of its force from a suspicion, engendered in part by the standard model of theory in the philosophy of science, that critical theory was not legitimately theoretical, and that "dialectical materialism" was more metaphysics than materialism (cf. Elster, 1985, and Roemer, 1985). It also drew upon a much reduced interpretation of Poulantzas's ambitious attempt to revitalize Marxism, which, as such, could hardly fail to drift in the direction of a positivist theory of rational choice and a hyper-sociological account of classes and the divergence of class interests. This sociology of class reduced the problem of the contradiction of the relations and forces of production to one of collective action in the interest of rectifying the injustices of the capitalist distribution of wealth, and it emphasized the rationality of pursuing individual goals by means of combining with others, e.g., in unions or parties. What was theoretical about this was either too positive for any political translation or too beholden to insights selected, to a large extent in opposition to their theoretical context, to the problem of eliminating the vestiges of metaphysics and other sources of vagueness thought to be associated with critical theory. The idea of rational choice was inadequate to the idea of the capitalist mode of production. The sociology of class differences, based on strictly economic criteria, also depended more on insight than theory, and while it offered something of a notion of politics, it remained mired in the institutionalist frame of reference in which conditions of rational action limit what could be conceived of as potentially effective political agency.[1] In regard to its generalizing aspirations, I believe that this mix of rational choice and a sociology of class structure has not yet shown that it can contribute much to our understanding of contemporary society, nor has it provided sufficient complexity in considering the relationship between political economy and sociology. It has also failed to provide what critical theory needs to provide, namely both a sense of what is wrong in what we claim to know about human affairs and a sense of what makes criticism possible as an immanent feature of human affairs. In other words, it amounts to a more rigorous way of sustaining a narrowly instrumentalist approach against the critical impulse, in theory and, as it turns out, in practice.

Surprisingly, there was a distinct but latent subjectivist emphasis in this approach, particularly in its individualistic version of rationality and its eventual decline into the idea of rational choice as a normative ideal rather than a theory. To that extent, it might have been included among the subjectivist tendencies of "western Marxism." The point is that insight took precedence over theory in this instance of the qualified reception of the texts of critical theory, including Marxism, and one part of its appeal was largely due to a belief, understandable in the last third of the twentieth century, that the most important task for radical intellectuals was to

---

[1]The concept of political effectiveness implicit in this had to do with outcomes rather than with, say, increasing the manifest features of the contradictions of capitalist production. While an argument can be made that if political agency is an issue, and if the last instance is not recent enough, then measurable outcomes are all that are relevant to thinking about effectiveness. Without a theory which goes beyond the insights it is difficult if not impossible to be sure whether or not the unanticipated consequences of one or another sort of action have the potential to be socially progressive.

establish either a viable theory of politics or a discourse devoted to the possibility of a new concept of democracy and a correspondingly new concept of politics. One can hardly fault that decision, given the circumstances and given recent history. But the point is not that it can be explained. It is, rather, that it was not based on a reception of theoretical work able to acknowledge what is theoretical about it, which is to say that it was not based on an interest in the crucial meta-theoretical question "what is critical about critical theory?"

Critical theory is systematic only to the extent to which it involves integrating its three important aspects, intention, form of argumentation, and conditions of validation. It is critical to the extent to which it is self-critical and mindful of the relation of theory to practice. Its major twentieth century classics, including *History and Class Consciousness* and *Dialectic of Enlightenment*, used language in a way that was unfamiliar to many sociologists and involved forms of argumentation and a philosophy which were equally unfamiliar. This accounts in part for why it was unable to insinuate itself into the main stream of American sociological thought, a particularly significant fact given the failure of structural functionalism to outlive its major protagonist, Talcott Parsons. Sociology was left, in effect, with the language and concepts of functionalism but without the theory which warranted the use of that language and the deployment of those concepts. Given the difficulty of engaging the European literature and given the apparent suitability of insight to the pressing problem of rethinking politics, the study of theories, a kind of mining for insights, began to replace the activity of theorizing. At the same time, largely through the imported works of, most notably, Roland Barthes, Julia Kristeva, Jacques Derrida, Paul de Man, Gilles Deleuze, and Michel Foucault, and by the writings of later scholars in the United States, such as Gayatri Chakravorty Spivak (1987), Judith Butler (1989), and Randy Martin (2002), the issue of how to sustain criticism in both the intellectual and political sense, and the more technical issue of how to integrate its three aspects, re-entered the field of the human sciences, largely but not exclusively through literary and cultural studies (cf. Grossberg, Nelson, and Treichler, 1991; Nelson and Grossberg, 1988; Greenblatt and Gunn, 1992). This is one context in which one can evaluate the works of the thinkers discussed by Professor Snedeker and appreciate his comments on them.

I believe that it is in regard to this conjuncture that he is more than justified in revisiting their works and attempting to understand their implications for our present situation and the relation of theory to practice which is appropriate to it. Of those implications, I have in mind two which are, in effect, normative. First is an obligation to reconsider what can be meant by "theory" and how that might relate to a well-formed idea of criticism. The second is an obligation to re-engage Marx's critique of political economy itself, not so much for what it is supposed to have said about the nature of capitalism, but for what it demonstrates about the nature of theory if criticism is to be an immanent feature of it (cf. Martin, 2002). Both obligations depend on a willingness to consider the special character of self-reflection in critical theory (cf. Blum and McHugh, 1984) and the relationship between a socio-politically valid concept of "criticism" and "society" as an essentially irreducible concept. Not all the authors discussed in this book directly address these obligations, but Professor Snedeker sustains a sense of the significance of their work in this regard to the literature of which they are part.

What may seem ironic about renewed interest in at least some of these figures is that they now seem important precisely for their bearing on the problem of politics, which was, at one time, the basis for skepticism about at least some of them. Given that globalization, however defined, requires a rethinking of politics particularly in regard to the complex and apparently irresistible forces set in motion as the basis of a qualitatively different, socially dysfunctional, "system," what Hardt and Negri call "empire," thinking about politics requires thinking about theory, and thinking about theory can only be worthwhile if theory involves more than insight and if one respects the complexity required if it is to be critical in the sense discussed above. It would be difficult for anyone seriously interested in the idea of a politics of resistance and opposition, in the context of what appears to be an extraordinarily coercive global transformation in favor of capital, to justify avoiding those authors reviewed by Professor Snedeker, as well as others in the greater tradition of criticism, critical studies, and critical theory.

It remains the case that there is some tension between Marxism and the general notion of critical theory, despite the fact that Marx's critique of capital remains, arguably, our most complete and influential example of such a theory. I have indicated some sources of this tension, emphasizing the fact that, until recently, Marxism has been typically rendered by American sociologists in an altogether reduced and over-simplified form, as with many other instances of critical thought (cf. Ollman, 1971, for a notable attempt to correct that tendency). The European-influenced mix of structuralism and critical theory remains crucial to current theorizing aimed at identifying the immanence of politics to post-productive capitalism, especially in regard to its emphases on representations, discourse, sociality, the circulation of people, cultural generativity, subjugation, power, and resistance.

This mix has oppositional aspects, and one sees evidence of this in Professor Snedeker's account of Habermas's rejection of "post-modernist" thought, a rejection based on the idea that without an established norm it is not possible, convincingly, to theorize democracy and/or to rationalize an authentically popular politics, and therefore not possible, again convincingly, to criticize authoritarianism, imperialism, and fascism. Yet, it seems clear that when the conception of politics is brought into line with conceptions of the current situation, the generative aspect of culture, the limits of representation, and critical theory, a wholesale assault on all that momentarily falls under the rubric of "post-modernism" is almost certain to be unhelpful. Raymond Williams and Edward Said, among the authors discussed by Professor Snedeker, understood this despite their uneasiness with what they see as the political vagueness and possibly reactionary tendencies of some instances of contemporary criticism.

Professor Snedeker's book represents an impressive attempt to recuperate some of what is in danger of being lost of the radical thought of the twentieth century, and to bring his account of these instances of critical theory to bear on the problem of relating theory to practice under conditions which provide a severe test of the radical imagination. His essays engage these thinkers in a kind of conversation in which the author's voice provides a counterpoint to their voices. The result is both an introduction to a number of important theorists whose works remain fundamental to contemporary thought (or should be considered fundamental), and a discussion of radical thinking at a time when the conditions of sustaining such a project seem at best precarious. These essays renew the debate over Perry Anderson's interpretation and characterization of "western Marxism" at a time when the older terms of the debate about communism no longer seem as compelling as they once were. Nor does it seem as easy as it had been to dismiss the emphasis on subjective aspects of society, especially those around the problem of political agency. Indeed, it is just the emphasis on politics, which all these authors share, which makes it possible to revisit the notion of culture and to distinguish between the subjective as politics and the subjective as mind. It is the latter which has been largely displaced by the former, giving the notion of subjectivity a more historical and materialist grounding than it might have been thought to have at the time of Anderson's writing. Professor Snedeker enlightens that distinction by rejecting the individualistic ontology that accompanied some versions of "western Marxism" while arguing that "subjective conditions" of society, e.g., culture and politics, can be understood within the historical perspective of classical Marxian theory.

BIBLIOGRAPHY

Anderson, Perry. 1978. *Considerations on Western Marxism*. London: New Left Books,.

Blum, Alan, and Peter McHugh. 1984. *Self-Reflection in the Arts and Sciences*. Atlantic Highlands, N.J.: Humanities.

Bogen, David. 1999. *Order Without Rules*. New York: SUNY Press.

Brown, Michael E., and Amy Goldin. 1973. *Collective Behavior*. Pacific Palisades: Goodyear.

Brown, Michael E. 1986. *The Production of Society*. Lanham, Md.: Rowman and Littlefield.

Butler, Judith. 1989. *Gender Trouble*. London: Routledge.

Elster, J. 1985. *Making Sense of Marx*. Cambridge, UK: Cambridge University Press.

Geuss, Raymond. 1981. *The Idea of Critical Theory: Habermas and the Frankfurt School*. Cambridge, UK: Cambridge University Press.

Greenblatt, Stephen, and Giles Gunn, eds. 1992. *Redrawing the Boundaries*. New York: The Modern Language Association of America.

Grossberg, Lawrence, Cary Nelson, and Paula Treichler, eds. 1991. *Cultural Studies*. London: Routledge.

Martin, Randy. 2002. *On Your Marx*. Minneapolis: University of Minnesota Press.

Nelson, Cary, and Lawrence Grossberg, eds. 1988. *Marxism and the Interpretation of Culture*. Champaign, IL: University of Illinois Press.

Nozick, Robert. 1981. *Philosophical Explanations*. Cambridge, MA: Harvard University Press.

Ollman, Bertell. 1971. *Alienation*. Cambridge, UK: Cambridge University Press.

Roemer, John, ed. 1985. *Analytical Marxism*. Cambridge, UK: Cambridge University Press.

Spivak, Gayatri Chakravorty. 1987. *In Other Worlds*. London: Methuen.

Sweezy, Paul. 1942. *The Theory of Capitalist Development*. New York: Monthly Review Press.

Wright, Erik Olin. 1989. *The Debate on Classes*. London: Verso.

PREFACE

My primary goal in writing the essays which comprise this book was to present a series of authors whose work was not well known to sociologists. I also wanted to broaden the definition of Critical Theory beyond the well-known association of this term with the work of the Frankfurt School. I felt that the work of Raymond Williams, Edward W. Said and that of George Lukacs after *History and Class Consciousness* was not well known by most sociologists and that Oliver C. Cox has been treated as a marginal figure in the history of the discipline.

The primary innovation of my research lies in its interdisciplinary approach to contemporary sociological theory. In the essays that follow I transgress the boundaries between sociology, literary criticism and philosophy. In this book, the term "Critical Theory" is given a double meaning. It refers to both the work of the Frankfurt School and other neomarxist social theorists as well as to recent work in literary criticism as this has been applied to the analysis of society.

My interest in literary criticism goes beyond cultural studies and the sociology of literature. Literary criticism is important to sociology because it brings to the forefront of debate the question of the ideology of the text, and it recognizes the rhetorical basis for interpretation and evaluation. I demonstrate that the link between culture and society is where ideology is both conveyed and contested. It is in this context that figures as diverse as Georg Lukacs, Edward W. Said and Raymond Williams become important to the project of a critical theory of society.

The first chapter of the book discusses the turn from political economy to cultural critique by the main figures of Western Marxism from Georg Lukacs, Theodor W. Adorno and Herbert Marcuse to Henri Lefebvre and Louis Althusser. In this chapter, I distinguish my own position from that of Perry Anderson in his *Considerations on Western Marxism*. The second chapter provides a discussion of Georg Lukacs's critique of philosophical irrationalism as it was expressed in his analysis of philosophy, literature and sociology. Chapter three addresses the literary criticism of Edward W. Said, particularly his critique of the ideology of Orientalism. This chapter also includes a discussion of Said's analysis of the political functions of criticism as a humanistic discourse. Chapter four deals with the cultural criticism of Raymond Williams. I locate Williams's work on the border of literary criticism and sociological theory as well as discuss his argument that culture is a form of politics. Chapter five deals with Jürgen Habermas's defense of modernity against what he sees as a new form of philosophical irrationalism in postmodern social theory. This has import since I argue that Habermas's work has more in common with that of Lukacs than most social theorists have been willing to grant. Chapter six provides a discussion of the critique of the ideology of racism as this was developed by Oliver C. Cox. For Cox, the analysis of racism took the form of a critique of the "caste analogy" of race relations. His alternative was to locate racism within the history of capitalism as a justification for the superexploitation of the black worker. This essay is also an attempt to revive interest in a largely forgotten radical voice in the history of sociology in the United States.

ACKNOWLEDGEMENTS

Several friends have helped me turn these essays into a book. Special thanks go to Mike Brown, Randy Martin, Frank Rosengarten, Sally Luther and John Neumaier. Without their intellectual and moral support, this book never would have seen the light of day.

CHAPTER 1

Western Marxism and the Problem of History

In this essay, I will develop a critique of the main tendencies within Western Marxism since World War II as exemplified by the work of Henri Lefebvre, Jürgen Habermas, Herbert Marcuse, and Louis Althusser. Since the familiar interpreter of this tradition is Perry Anderson, I will begin by summarizing his account and establishing my own in contrast to it. My argument is, essentially, that the ungoverned theoretical contradiction of Western Marxism is its insistence upon an ontological theory of human nature and its failure to reconcile that theory with adequate conceptions of historical development and mode of production. Ultimately, I argue that such a reconciliation is not possible in the terms set by the Western Marxist debate, and that any further development of the relation between the subjective and objective conditions of society will have to return, in one way or another, to the historical perspective of classical Marxian theory.

The Western Marxist Adventure

The phrase "Western Marxism" was first used by Maurice Merleau-Ponty (1973) in his *Adventures of the Dialectic*. He used it to identify a group of theorists concerned with the problematic of subjectivity that had been emphasized by Marx, yet curiously rejected in the "orthodox" Marxism of the communist parties. The themes of this problematic were culture, consciousness, and everyday life. Merleau-Ponty was well aware of what was, and continues to be, at stake in this debate:

> If we have undertaken to recall Lukacs's attempt (very freely, and emphasizing certain points in his work were only indicated), it is because something of it remains in today's Marxism or even because it is one of those truths which only by chance miss the historical record. We shall

see, on the contrary, that there was something justified in the opposition
it encountered. But it was necessary to recall this lively and vigorous
attempt, in which the youth of revolution and Marxism lives again, in
order to measure today's communism, to realize what it has renounced
and to what it has resigned itself. (Merleau-Ponty 1973, 57-78)

Nevertheless, while it is not entirely clear what he held the full theoretical
contribution of "Western Marxism" to be, Merleau-Ponty's use of the
phrase served quite well to indicate a range of theoretical orientations
quite at odds with that of the orthodox Marxists, and a shift away from
the economism of the latter toward sociocultural studies.

Marxists are still interested in the question of how to reconcile an
epistemologically defensible cultural analysis with a more traditional
political economy. For Merleau-Ponty, the problem was that both were
equally fundamental and that communist Marxism had eliminated the
former in favor of the latter. The result was a degeneration of theory in
the directions of economic reductionism and a methodology entirely too
mechanistic to do justice to the dynamism of history and the subtlety of
social order found in the Western capitalist nations.

Perry Anderson's Critique of Western Marxism

Perry Anderson's (1976) use of the phrase is not directed specifically at
the same problems of the relationship of base to superstructure and material
life to culture. Nor is it intended to make the case that materialism has
come to deny the historical force of culture. Instead, and on the contrary,
he stresses the exaggerations that began to characterize the new orthodoxies
of "critical theory," as culture and consciousness became dominant themes
in the literature of European neo-Marxism from 1918-1968.

Where Merleau-Ponty emphasized the problems of a one-sided
political economy, Anderson points to the problems of a one-sided theory
of culture and consciousness. Rather than treat this as no more than an
intellectual defect, one that could be repaired by right thinking, Anderson
tries to place it in the historical context of a depoliticized scholarly left,
exiled to the academy, unable to assimilate the "failures" of the workers'
movements, and detached from or hostile to the politics of socialism. The
authors whose works are the resources for this discussion are, among
others, Lukacs, Korsch, Adorno, Horkheimer, Marcuse, Habermas, Sartre,
Lefebvre, Althusser, and Colletti. His solution is Trotsky, insofar as
Trotsky's influence is understood as requiring detailed case studies of the
history of proletarian revolutionary movements and the formations they

have opposed.

Consistent with his argument, Anderson attempts to show the more general historical conditions of Western Marxism and the corresponding problems it addressed, and the institutional limitations of the academic disciplines upon the further development of historical materialism. The conditions and political problems have to do with the Russian Revolution, the rise of Fascism, and the apparent hegemony achieved by the capitalist class by the middle of the twentieth century. The institutional limitations have to do with the ghettoization of Marxism, the elevation of philosophy as the Marxian paradigm, and the practical divorce of intellectuals from the workers' movement. The urgency of the former and the ambiguities inherent in the latter contributed to a one-sided analysis of society, compatible with divisions among academicized disciplines, as well as to the hermetic quality of much of the writing of that tradition and the vagueness and theoreticism with which Anderson seems to believe it is, more often than not, afflicted.

The return to Trotsky is, then, not merely Anderson's solution to the intellectual problem, but the correction of the political defect. It is also the way in which he believes intellectual work can be reconciled with the praxis of the working class. This is clear from Anderson's list of "insistent" issues to which contemporary Marxists must address themselves:

> What is the constitutive nature of bourgeois democracy? What is the function and future of the nation-state? What is the real character of imperialism as a system? What is the historical meaning of a workers' state without workers' democracy? How can a socialist revolution be made in the advanced capitalist countries? How can internationalism be made a genuine practice, not merely a pious ideal? How can the fate of previous revolutions in comparable conditions be avoided in the ex-colonial countries? How can established systems of bureaucratic privilege and oppression be attacked and abolished? What would be the structure of an authentic socialist democracy? These are the great unanswered problems that form the most urgent agenda for Marxist theory today (Anderson 1976, 121).

A depressing agenda, since it seems to say that anything short of this degree of comprehensiveness must, given the urgency, represent total failure. On the other hand, the list can only be programmatic if it is taken as a cue to move to deeper theoretical issues, perhaps issues at the core of Marxism and at the core of Perry Anderson's own apparent absolutism in the final passage of his book.

The Question of Theory and Practice

Yet, to raise the theoretical problem again seems to place one among the writers who have abandoned politics and history. Somehow, it is necessary to recapture the urgency of theoretical work without falling between the cracks made by the uneven development of the workers' movement, or, in the alternative, without reducing theory to matters of strategy alone. Anderson, however, seems to have thrown out the one in favor of the other.

To put it simply, Anderson's criticism of the Western Marxists is a practical one: their work is irrelevant to a progressive or revolutionary movement. In this, he seems to be arguing either for a theory devised within the specific strategic contexts of revolutionary action, or one that contains within itself an adequate strategy for revolution whether or not a movement exists as such. If the former, then Marx himself can be condemned; if the latter, there is no way of gauging the relevance of the theory except through utopian speculation.

The problem is that Anderson has been able to locate a theoreticism within the Marxist tradition, but has failed to discover its internal cause. The failure, he seems to say, is a result of non-theoretical and easily remediable choices of perspective, political preference, and alliance, rather than something intrinsic to the theoretic formulations themselves that might even stem from an ambiguity in the classical Marxian texts. He seems to deny the legitimacy of critique in favor of case study, and hence seems to take entirely too much for granted so far as theory is concerned. In fact, at the heart of Anderson's complaint may be precisely the sort of theoreticism he seems to decry, disguised, as it were, by the deceptively immediate plausibility of the final questions that make up his agenda.

I want to show, for the same theorists listed as members of the tradition of Western Marxism, the intellectual basis of their practical irrelevance. The value of this inquiry lies, beyond its disclosure of a fundamental meta-theoretical problem, in its capacity to make a case for the relative autonomy of theoretical work within the epistemological requirements of an adequate relation of theory and practice.

If this is so, then one need not reject as elitist the use of technical language in theoretical works, condemn altogether the apparent distance of theoretical formulations from strategic considerations, or lament without hope the institutional isolation of Marxist scholarship. To return to "history" at the most fundamental level of theory is, *ipso facto*, a return to relevance. What then can be discussed are the mediations of that achievement—the ways in which theorists and their work become implicated in real organizational politics, a problem not addressed in this essay but of obvious significance if my central argument holds.

Subjectivity and Production

In order to retain the significance of the subjective within the framework of historical materialism, it is necessary to re-examine the concept of the mode of production within the context of the forces and relations that account for the contemporary reproduction of capitalist society. Because of its comprehensiveness to this very project, classical Marxian theory is at the very least a reasonable point of departure and one for which no equally comprehensive alternative theory has yet been devised.

It is appropriate to identify "classical" Marxism with the "classical" Marxian text, the first volume of *Capital*. This is the most complete and authoritative statement of Marx's mature position. Its analysis is familiar; the central focus is capitalist production. This provides a concept adequate to the analysis of the totality of capitalist society and to a history of the social relations by which capitalism develops. Colletti has summarized Marx's definition of capitalist society in terms of the specific characteristics of class relations within the mode of production:

> The historical subject then is neither Idea, World-Spirit, Vico's Providence, nor a transcendental subject. Nor is the subject conceived as Evolution, Struggle for Existence, Societal Instinct, Race, etc. Against these generic abstractions, all equally fruitless, Marx produces a new concept of the subject as a historical-natural entity, as a species or collectivity of empirical formation—such, precisely, as are social classes (Colletti 1972, 14).

This gives analytic, but by no means necessarily empirical, priority to politics and economics rather than to culture, and methodological priority to action rather than to ideas. In its reversal of these priorities, Western Marxism, as Anderson describes it, has lost its capacity to clarify the distinctiveness of capitalism and the significance of the class relations that the Western Marxists nevertheless insisted, in their asides, were fundamental to capitalism and its transformation. They were left with the abstractions of domination and liberation and an implicit philosophical anthropology placed, by virtue of the moralism of these abstractions, beyond suspicion.

This reversal finally gained intellectual support from an emphasis on language, consciousness, and everyday life. It is doubtless one of the virtues of Western Marxism that it has restored subjectivity to the Marxian tradition. But it has floundered on the untheorized conception of human nature, or essence, that it formulated to legitimate that interest. The result has been an ahistorical view of capitalism and a romantic view of history. It is not only that Being has replaced Becoming, but human nature has insinuated itself, replacing collective action, as the bed-rock of a history without historical dynamism. In their extended formulations, the Western Marxist analyses of language, consciousness, and everyday life— subjectivity—are ontological in a way that departs markedly from the Marxism of *Capital*, and from the enduring Marxist critique of idealism and ideology. The subtle projection by the Western Marxists of an ontology of human nature had the immediate effect of preventing an epistemological solution to the problem of the relation of theory and practice and therefore an historical materialist theory of society. This, rather than a choice of perspective, political preference, and alliance, is their ungoverned contradiction.

Social change, understood by classical Marxism as epistemologically central to historical materialism, required that social phenomena be understood in connection with the existing mode of social and material production, itself taken as a product of struggle within and in relation to material life. From that point of view, consciousness in capitalist society was part of class relations and thus was inevitably divided, volatile, and in process. Neither consciousness nor the everyday life which was its local and temporary realization could be, in this view, autonomous or a reflection of a universal human essence without obliterating the very notion of history as human activity and collective accomplishment.

For an adequate Marxist formulation of subjectivity, including everyday life, consciousness, and language, there would have to be a recognition of the centrality to those topics of the historical transformation and reconstitution of class relations. As is well known, this involves building analytic links to the contradictions of the existing forces and relations of production, with a focus on the relations of commodity production and capitalist accumulation. These class relations and contradictions constitute, as a theoretical matter, the capitalist mode of production. They define both its internal logic, capital accumulation through the exploitation of labor, and its historical dynamic, the incessant tensions of class struggle.

According to this formulation, neither the accumulation of capital nor the existence of class struggle, nor contradiction itself, can be viewed as independent factors shaping modern society. They are, instead, themselves determinate aspects of the structure and history of the capitalist mode of production. The labor theory of value attempts rigorously to establish the relationship between accumulation and exploitation on the one hand, and the contradiction of production and society on the other. And it does this within the conceptual limitations required by the relation of theory and practice in Marxist epistemology.

Analyzing capitalism in terms of the development and internal logic of production does not exclude the analysis of subjectivity. Nor does it inhibit or necessarily distort the analyses of language, consciousness, or everyday life. In fact, all three were central to Marx's critique of capitalism. Consider the importance he placed upon alienation, fetishism, and reification. But it must be stressed that these concepts are specific to the analysis of the ramifications of capitalist production and are not simply the result of a prior insight into human affairs divorced from their history and the history of theory itself. "Fetishism" refers specifically to the fetishism of the commodity, "alienation" to the obligatory and unconditional sale of labor power on the capitalist market, and "reification" to one aspect of the subjective side of universal commodity exchange.

From the perspective of classical Marxism, everyday life, consciousness, and language must be identified and analyzed in relation to the existing mode of production and its local realizations and variations. In turn, subjectivity must be formulated as a feature of the historical process of the development of the capitalist mode of production as a whole, as a feature of its necessary social relations, rather than as an empirical category that specifies data to which theory must then conform.

The Abandonment of Classical Marxism by Habermas, Lefebvre, Marcuse and Althusser

In one way or another, the Western Marxists have minimized or abandoned the concept of the mode of production as the key to socio/historical analysis. Occasionally, this is a matter of theoretic principle, as with some writers who have been influenced by Lefebvre. More often, it is an abandonment *de facto*, in which society and economy are placed at so great a conceptual distance from one another that their relationship ceases to provide any basis whatsoever for practical representation. The dominance of the economic and its historical operation "in the last instance" become, at best, formalisms in which the position of that "last instance," and therefore the economic itself, can no longer be represented in concrete research. What is lost, finally, is the determinate character of society and its aspects. Economy comes, instead, at best, to indicate a notion of finality that is cosmological, since it has become a "last instance" only when every other "instance" is said and done.

HABERMAS

The work of Habermas (1975), despite early and casual acknowledgment of the conflict of classes, represents the latter sort of departure from classical Marxism. Communication and the imperatives of system and social "integration" provide Habermas with a theory adequate to his description of "late capitalism," and, to some extent, with an account of an historical process. But the contradiction of system and social integration (policy and consensus) that he attempts to establish as the basis of his account only explains crisis at the level of policy. It accounts for little more than policy and the ephemerae of social movements. There is no notion of struggle and none of revolution possible in this formula. Human beings are read out of history because groups are excluded as a matter of theoretic principle. What is left is an extra-human subjectivity, a discursive agency that makes history by reading it, and presumably by being read. Inevitably, historical agency makes its appearance as media, channels, dialogue, and an intellectual elite, and one is thrown back to the idealism that Marx had so long ago laid to rest.

Or the dynamic of social change is ultimately found by psychology, where the distortion of communication lies in the incompatibility of the message with the irrepressibility of human need. Liberation is, then, to be found in the ideal speech situation, the dialogue, that is presumed by all communication, distorted or not; and the dominated is definitely not something that feels the weight of power, wealth, and capital. It suffers and works only in the abstract. Habermas mistakes logical conditions of speaking (exchange) with a domain of being (intersubjectivity) underlying in fact every speech act. Thus, in this sense, there is tautology at the heart of his analysis of freedom that makes the idea of freedom itself suspect. Moreover, the theory that provided a philosophical basis for recognizing the corruption of language, the Marxist critique of ideology, is ignored, as if that corruption is obvious to anyone who would look, listen, and feel. Thus the conditon of making sense of Habermas's notions of domination and liberation is a theory, Marxism, for which he makes no discernible place in his account of late capitalism; either his work is a microanalysis, in which case the hard work of connecting it to Marxism has yet to be done, or it is *ad hoc*, in which case, he needs to begin again.

It is true that Habermas develops his perspective out of an interpretation of classical Marxism, as entirely too instrumentalist to account for the forms of cultural life and social hegemony characteristic of late capitalism. In any case, the result is an intuitively-based emphasis upon freedom taken as essential to all successful human development, an expressive theory of need-governed communication that begs entirely too many questions, and an unjustified yet appealing idea of an emancipatory human interest capable of motivating social change through a praxis that has no clear historical force. His interpretation of Marx is so convenient to the characterization of late capitalism as posing a problem of communication, that one suspects that Habermas projected his Marx from the standpoint of a society the description of which he was already led to by an unaccountably casual methodology. The psychological reduction necessary for a theory of change based on the repression of need begs, as well, the problem of power, and with that the historical role of classes, collectivities, systems, empires, and modes of production.

Above all, the return to a vitalist essentialism, and ontology of human nature, bodes ill for the development within Habermas's thought of an adequate description and a genuine history of late capitalism. The archaic stage theory presented in his (1975) *Legitimation Crisis* is no more than a preliminary outline of an approach to such a history, at best of vaguely heuristic and pedagogical value. Habermas leaves his readers with too much psychology, an ontology of human nature, not enough history, and a methodology that substitutes the illustration of an idea for a rigorous historical materialism.

LEFEBVRE

"Need" also figures in Lefebvre's (1971) most popular works, where it serves to identify a source of ambivalence in everyday life: one acts, but cannot tell whether the act flows from need or is a result of external norm or imposition. Lefebvre's influence among the situationists and some Freudian Marxists has been largely in the direction of a subjectivist reductionism whose intelligibility relies on an allegory of the violation of human nature by a guilty social order. This is more the expression of moral indignation and outrage than an historical materialism of capitalist society. Like Habermas, Lefebvre explicated his ontology through a set of familiar empirical studies—of consumerism, urbanism, mass communication, the corruption of leisure, and bureaucracy. Change reflects an upsurge of expression by human nature, or it represents the success of an unnamed therapeutic intervention. The assumption of abundance, and with it the arbitrariness of any control over need—from there a short way to "Anti-Oedipus and the hero-schizo-phrene" (Deleuse and Guattari, 1977) — is possible only on condition that radical political economy has become irrelevant as a fact and as theory.

Both Habermas and Lefebvre place human nature prior to capitalism. Their metaphorical figure, so familiar to the hopeful, nostalgic, and then cynical politics of non-radical reform is "the quality of life." Instead of developing new historical categories justifying their rejection of the mode of production, and instead of acknowledging historical limits to analysis itself, they employ ontological categories to account for the most general sort of liberatory movement conceivable. This relies on several interdependent assumptions: that an adequate theory of social change must begin with the absolute and empirically interpretable poles of domination and liberation; that prior movements toward socialism have therefor failed to liberate people, not from within capitalism or feudalism, but totally; that the dynamic of social change cannot be in capitalism but must be in people regardless of where they find themselves; and, that an adequate theory of social change must grade revolutionary movements by their immediately visible results and by the most obvious forms they take. Thus a desire to develop a theory of total liberation, the reliance on an interpretation of Marxism as instrumentalist, and a consequent identification of areas in which the project of devising liberation can be fulfilled without what is normally taken to be praxis, characterize the plunge into an ontology of human nature, and with it, in some cases, cynicism and/or a politics of the gut or the mind.

MARCUSE

Herbert Marcuse (1964) shared some of these same concerns and problems. Consciousness, domination, and liberation are the figures of his drama without history. His conception of consciousness is grounded in his interpretation and sociological transformation of Freudian psycho-analysis. For Marcuse, this expresses the transhistorical nature of human consciousness. His conception of emancipation depends on the possibility of the total emancipation of the libido from a repressive social order. Late capitalism is distinctive only by virtue of being the most repressive, yet least coercive, society, a society of indefinite scale and infinitely reduced dimension. Yet, Marcuse's refusal to give up on praxis, displaced to the margins of the material order and rendered exemplary, marks a difference from the more strict idealism of most of the other Western Marxists. But a politics of opposition cannot provide the articles of praxis necessary for an account of domination and liberation consistent with a theory of capitalist development and compatible with the historical possibility of such a theory. If Lefebvre and Habermas were excessively subjectivist, Marcuse, despite his use of psychology, has lost both subjectivity and objectivity. Analysis drifts undialectically between the poles of disparate action and an unavoidable domination. Here, it is both of these that are granted absolute Being, rather than human nature by itself.

Marcuse's position is more useful to historical materialism than that of Habermas or Lefebvre. It does not deny the significance of social conflict. Nor does it leave conflict as a merely formal operation. It does not obliterate, though it leaves obscure, the dynamic of capitalism and the relevance of capitalism to the existence of the most familiar forms of repression and strife. Marcuse's work serves classical Marxism by its elaborate though idealized description of an unimpeded and monolithic capitalist control. There, capitalism does what Marx supposed it could never do: it completes itself. At the same time, Marcuse leaves room for political struggle and therefore some sort of history. Nevertheless, like the work of Lefebvre and Habermas, his can only be comprehended as part of an analysis of history if it is placed within the more familiar Marxist formulations. Otherwise, domination is inexplicable, and the universal interest in liberation becomes an ideal. Its major use can only be the rejection of all past instances of struggle, all incomplete or inchoate acts of resistance within capitalism, all forms of class struggle. Otherwise, critical theory as what would be left of Marxism would become hostile to its own possibility and, perhaps, finally reactionary.

ALTHUSSER

It is significant that one stream of Western Marxism derives from an explicit reliance on the labor theory of value. Yet, perhaps because of the desire of its major figures to do too much too soon, to counter all manner of modern idealism on the left in one fell swoop, it too succumbs to an ontology—this time of levels, practices, and practitioners. That stream derives from the work of Althusser (1977) and his early associates. On the surface, it appears diametrically opposed to the rest of what has here been referred to as Western Marxism. Where the others speak of literature, culture, and society, Althusser speaks of practices, apparatuses, and a history (and therefore, presumably, a social order) devoid of subjectivity. Where they speak of and do philosophy, he invokes the spirit of science and objectivity capable of closing in on final truths, or at least finally refuting falsehood. Along the way, Althusser raises the fundamental critical question that must be asked of the Western Marxists: if what is important is subjectivity, in the form stated, and if what is of greatest practical urgency is the freeing of individual subjects, in what way is the Marxist version of these problems distinct from other versions and approaches? What has Marx told us that is new?

Despite criticisms of his strategy for addressing this question, criticisms of a primarily historiographic form that argue with his periodizations of Marx's writings into immature and mature stages, the question remains a serious one. And this is so regardless of one's position on the status and significance of Althusser's thought. Yet, the extreme character of Althusser's own response has left a legacy of scientism, positivism, and a fairly standard idealism of reason and its putative agencies. On the other hand, it seems to be a gain over revolutionary idealism, the idealism of the adventure, to state that history has no subject. But is it a gain for Marxism? It is so only if "history" refers to totality and structure rather than to dynamism and process. Althusser's "discovery" is not, then, a result of a clearer reading of Marx (in the light of Saussure), but a redefinition of the term "history" that, itself, constitutes a radical departure from the dialectical character of historical materialism. Althusser wants history, but only one that Marx himself rejected—the succession of events along an absolute time line. He wants History without history, just as the humanists he decries want Change without change. He is left with an ontology of the whole, and in justification of theory, an ontology of scientific reason. The latter discloses the former; but to whom? Not only history, but reason as well, lacks subjectivity. Althusser ends without a real subject because he began without a real history.

The virtue of his work lies in its devastatingly critical character, and in the fact that it continually provokes his readers with questions of great moment. But its flaw is so deep that it cannot be relevant to anything that one might suppose to be praxis, something of which Althusser himself expressed a nagging but marginal awareness. When the attempt is made to transform Althusserian Marxism into politically relevant theory, the Marxism withers away. One sees this clearly in the works of Hindess and Hirst (1977), in the extreme skepticism that reflects the unhappiness of a consciousness for whom reason is both necessary and beyond its grasp.

Conclusion
Classical Marxism establishes an objective conception of human subjectivity compatible with the requirements of historical materialism and adequate to the analysis of capitalism and its transformation. While

the burden remains to show its capacity to comprehend the present situation, the possibility can no longer be denied in advance. In fact, it is the collapse of Western Marxism that brings us back to the question of value, classes, exploitation, uneven development, and the specific contradictions of capitalism, early or late.

Western Marxism, motivated by the difficulty of reconciling theory with the practice of the parties and by the dread of fascism, nevertheless found itself possessed of an intuitionist methodology and a subjectivism incompatible with the recognition of the role of social forces and relations in history. It had been led to its critique by Marxism, and led by its critique to deny Marxism in all respects. It could no longer explain its own development, due to this attempt to divorce itself from its origins. It always relied on literary strategies to demonstrate insight but inevitably found itself without grounds and without a sense of its own, as well as everything else's, historicity. In losing track of its way, it finally lost its point.

Nevertheless, Western Marxism has left a legacy of terms, problems, and concepts that have revived a concern with the theoretical representation of resistance and opposition, and an interest in the basic works of Marxism and their philosophical underpinnings. Moreover, it has provided the most sustained and elaborate critique of capitalist culture and politics in the modern literature of social studies. The attempt to move beyond those accomplishments, to find a more general sociology than Marx and Marxism seemed to have provided, fell victim to the overly strong formulae, ontological, psychological, structuralist, that were, perhaps, necessary to regain the critical sensibility during the first two-thirds of the twentieth century. What had been gained in the appreciation of suffering and in the phenomenology of domination was, however, lost when Western Marxism attempted to read its literature as theory. That this would occur among such an otherwise diverse group may seem odd; yet it is less so when we consider what had come to be at stake for all of them, as us: the possibility of critique, of radical transformation, of Marxism, in the context of what all recognized as a capitalism of previously unimagined power, scale, and freedom.

How are we to evaluate Western Marxism since World War II? One possibility would be to discard the whole tradition as representing a regression to a pre-Marxist idealism. Anderson seems to follow this route. However, this overlooks the relationship between social theory and its history, as Anderson did even as he acknowledged that relationship. The subjectivist, and ultimately utopian, vision of Western Marxism was developed in relation to the political circumstances and historical conditions of the post-war period. Western Marxism is, itself, a product of late capitalism whose scale and pace of development could not help but raise questions about all theory, including Marxism, as well as it should.

Western Marxism cannot be understood outside of this context. Its development and formulation of an analysis of late capitalism was embedded within a cold war ideology and language over which it had little control. It attempted to transcend the structures of its situation by means of an ontologically grounded social theory. It is this that accounts for the isolation of Marxism under the auspices of the Western Marxists, for the ghettoization, the lack of connection with working class movements, the hermetic quality of the work, and the elitism and utopianism of both method and vision.

To be sure, the formulation of a language of resistance, for which Marcuse must be given the major credit, had a progressive role in the context of the social crises of the 1960s. However, the economic crisis of the 1970s and the political crisis of the 1980s have cast doubt on the capacity of a subjectivist critical theory to play an informing and strategic role in the struggles to come. What now appears to be a global crisis of capital, no longer merely the domination of consciousness in the industrial nations, has made class a crucial concept once again; and with it, the status of classical Marxism is being reevaluated in the light of the philosophical requirements of an historical materialism. One sees this in an enormous literature, divided and argumentative though it may be, accumulating in a variety of fields, and in the richness of the argumentation by which that literature is characterized. Culture and everyday life are no longer represented merely as areas of individual experience, but as arenas of struggle—in studies of language, media, child development, social organization, law, and social movements. (Ollman and Vernoff have provided a useful survey of some of the relevant literature, 1982; see also Raymond Williams, 1977.)

One is tempted to conclude that Western Marxism accomplished more in its demise than it had in its early and isolated appearance. Its strain toward a final conception of human affairs, its eclecticism, and the sheer weight of its pages, made it a force with which to contend, all the more so in the context of what now appears to be a world-wide struggle against capitalism, this time from within the global capital. What it finally accomplished for Marxism in this context is a more reflective return to a newly historical materialism and a subject-object dialectic of political economy capable of dealing with the global volatility of what continues to be the uneven development of capitalism.

REFERENCES

Althusser, Louis. 1977. *For Marx.* London: New Left Books.

Anderson, Perry. 1976. *Considerations on Western Marxism*. London: New Left Books. 121.

Colletti, Lucio. 1972. *From Rousseau to Lenin*. New York: Monthly Review Press 14.

Deleuze, Gilles and Guattari, Felix. 1977. *Anti-Oedipus*. New York: Viking.

Habermas, Jürgen. 1975. *Legitimation Crisis.* Boston: Beacon Press.

Hindess, Mary, Hirsch, Paul et al. 1977. *Marx's Capital and Capitalism Today*. London: Routledge and Kegan Paul.

Lefebvre, Henri. 1971. *Everyday Life in the Modern World*. New York: Harper Torch Books.

Marcuse, Herbert. 1964. *One Dimensional Man.* Boston: Beacon Press.

Merleau-Ponty, Maurice. 1973. *Adventures of the Dialectic*. Chicago: Northwestern.

Ollman, Bertell and Vernoff, Edward (eds.). 1982. *The Left Academy*. New York: McGraw-Hill.

Williams, Raymond. 1977. *Marxism and Literature*. London: Oxford University Press.

CHAPTER 2

The Politics of Epistemology: Georg Lukacs and the Critique of Irrationalism

History and Class Consciousness (Lukacs 1971a) is the canonical text of Western Marxism. In it Georg Lukacs opposed the mechanistic materialism of the Second International through the articulation of a Hegelian Marxism. The radical feature of *History and Class Consciousness* was its insistence upon the methodological primacy of the concept of totality and the centrality of culture to politics. Although this analysis was transformed by the Frankfurt School and the later disciples of Critical Theory into the critique of domination, the emphasis upon culture remained the key paradigm for Western Marxism.

With the exception of specialists in literary criticism (Jameson 1971, Ch. 3) contemporary discussions of Georg Lukacs typically praise the theoretical contribution of *History and Class Consciousness* to Western Marxism but deny any significance to his writings after 1930—accepting Isaac Deutscher's opinion (Deutscher 1971, 2113-93) that Lukacs had become a philosophical defender of Stalin's policies. *The Young Lukacs and the Origins of Western Marxism* by Andrew Arato and Paul Breines is a clear example of this point of view (Arato and Breines 1979). For Arato and Breines revolutionary Marxism received theoretical expression in the 1920s in the writings of Georg Lukacs and Karl Korsch and in the 1930s and '40s by the Frankfurt School and the French existentialists. This view of Lukacs has its explicit origin in Maurice Merleau-Ponty's chapter on Western Marxism in his *Adventures of the Dialectic* (Merleau-Ponty 1973), where he praised the cultural analysis of *History and Class Consciousness* in opposition to later developments in Communist thought. Important histories of the Frankfurt School (Jay 1973) and French Existentialism (Poster 1975) have accepted this distinction. The leading members of the Frankfurt School and the French existentialists did in fact virtually ignore Lukacs's writings after 1930.

In 1928, Lukacs published his "Blum Theses" (Lukacs 1972a, 227-53), in which he argued for a united front for the Hungarian Communist Party. He was in opposition to the position taken by the Comintern from 1928 to 1935, which viewed liberals and social democrats as social fascists. Although Lukacs wrote a self-criticism of his own position, he believed it to be correct. Seeing the fate that had befallen Karl Korsch, he viewed his self-criticism of his own position as a public posture which would prevent him from being expelled from the Party—in his opinion the only viable organization through which fascism might be opposed.

After 1928 Lukacs withdrew from administrative party work and wrote on literature and philosophy. His primary aim was to articulate the progressive elements within bourgeois culture in opposition to the reactionary tendencies which had become dominant. During the period from the 1930s through the 1950s, he developed an analysis of bourgeois irrationalism, the most important text being *The Destruction of Reason* (Lukacs 1981). *The Young Hegel* represents an attempt to reconstitute an alternative to the traditions of European philosophical development analyzed in *The Destruction of Reason*. Consider for example the following passage from the 1954 preface to a new edition of *The Young Hegel*:

> My account of the development of the young Hegel supplements in many respects the ideas I have attempted to formulate in my other studies of the history of German philosophy and literature. Above all the present work contains a positive vision to contrast with the "classical" age of irrationalism as presented in my work *The Destruction of Reason*. In that book I examined the irrationalist tradition established by Schelling and his successors. Here I shall be concerned with the critique and overcoming of irrationalism as seen from Hegel's side (Lukacs 1975, xi)...

The polemical aim of *The Young Hegel,* written in 1938 but not published until 1948, was to free Hegel from prevailing irrationalist interpretations by pro-Nazi philosophers in Germany.

Lukacs's analysis of irrationalism combines an analysis of the social function of ideas with an immanent critique. For Lukacs, this approach is necessary in order to prevent lapsing into either mechanistic materialism or idealism. In his view, an analysis which is based solely on the social function of ideas risks the danger of mechanistic materialism, and one which is based solely on an immanent critique risks the danger of idealism.

His conception of a dialectical analysis assumes the methodological necessity of the interaction between philosophy and historical development.

Lukacs did not provide a systematic formulation of his own philosophical perspective. Most of his writings during the period from the 1930s through the 1950s took the form of specific literary and philosophical studies, lacking an explicit and comprehensive summary of the argument that unites them. My primary effort in this essay is to summarize Lukacs's analysis of irrationalism. I briefly discuss his analyses of literature, philosophy, the Frankfurt School, and French existentialism, and his self-critique of the 1960s. In the concluding section I offer some critical remarks about the coherence and epistemological adequacy of this analysis and attempt to formulate Lukacs's own philosophical alternative to the traditions he rejects.

Literature as Ideology

In his studies of literature Lukacs conceives ideology as the world-view underlying an author's work. Although he rejects a mechanistic conception of the substructure-superstructure relation, he nevertheless asserts a determinism in which ideology has its origin in conditions of life. In his view, nihilism, cynicism, despair and angst are spontaneous products of capitalist society as a whole. At the same time, he suggests that bourgeois intellectuals have the responsibility to struggle against these tendencies of modern life and that they can do this by committing themselves to the practice of reason and the ideal of human progress (Lukacs 1963, 90-91). The problem with this position is that it fails to theorize the relationship between social determinism and the moral choice imputed to intellectuals.

This is the context in which Lukacs formulates the categories of naturalism, modernism, and critical realism. It is in terms of this problematic that critical realism is said to be preferable to both naturalism and modernism. Naturalism is criticized even when it expresses overt sympathies for the oppressed, as in the writings of Emile Zola and Upton Sinclair. It is criticized because it divorces subjective experience from its social conditions and formulates a mechanistic conception of social causation (Lukacs 1972b, 86-89). Literary naturalism is analogous to positivism in its inability to formulate a dialectical relationship between subjective experience and the external world (Lukacs 1963, 119).

For Lukacs, socialist realism was never anything more than an officially sanctioned naturalism (Lukacs 1969, 17). In his view it was analogous to the one-dimensionality of mechanistic materialism. He praised the work of Maxim Gorky because it embodied the perspective of critical realism more than that of socialist realism (Lukacs 1972b, 265-74). His positive evaluation of Balzac, Tolstoy and Thomas Mann was a protest against both bourgeois modernism and the mediocrity of the official Soviet literature under Stalin.

In Lukacs's view, literary modernism also produces the separation between subjective experience and its social conditions. It makes a fetish of the self and denies the existence of the objective world. Modernist writers (Kafka and Beckett are typical examples) substitute a conception of the absolute self and deny both history and personal biography (Lukacs 1963, 21). In separating subjective experience from the social world, they express a static conception of subjectivity, and the dissolution of personality is represented as an eternal human condition (Lukacs 1963, 26). The consequence of this world view is a conception of the world as fundamentally chaotic and unintelligible, which leads to a sense of despair and hopelessness; the possibility of human progress is no longer conceivable.

Naturalism and modernism are rejected because they deny the interaction between experience and social reality. The former reifies objectivity and the latter reifies subjectivity. In both cases the possibility of social development and progress through collective action is denied. Naturalism provides us with a mechanistic conception of the evolution of society, and modernism excludes the possibility of bettering the human condition altogether. Lukacs's alternative is the subject-object dialectic which he believes receives expression in critical realism:

> True great realism thus depicts man and society as complete entities, instead of showing merely one or the other of their aspects. Measured by this criterion, artistic trends determined by either exclusive intro-spection or exclusive extraversion equally impoverish and destroy reality (Lukacs 1972b, 6).

What is central to critical realism is its ability to depict social existence as a historical totality:

> Perspective, in this concrete form, is central to our problem. For there is an intimate connection between a writer's ability to create lasting human types (the real criterion of literary achievement) and his allegiance to an ideology which allows a belief in social development. Any attempt to substitute a static immobilism for the dynamic movement of history

must reduce the significance, the universality of the typology in question (Lukacs 1963, 57).

Here, perspective refers to a principle of selection, which enables an author to depict chaos as historically grounded. It is the presence of this perspective which makes Thomas Mann in Lukacs's view superior to all of the modernist writers of the 20th century (Lukacs 1964a).

Central to this discussion is the issue of the moral responsibility of intellectuals. Lukacs argues that intellectuals can make a choice between reason and irrationalism, between progress and decadence. They either allow themselves to be overwhelmed by chaos, cynicism and despair or they resist these tendencies in modern life by committing themselves to reason. While modernist writers submit to the decadent forces which are propelled by monopoly capitalism, critical realists express through literature the will to resist and overcome both personal angst and social chaos. What is of fundamental importance here is the relationship between social crisis and an author's moral and political commitments.

The Critique of Philosophical Irrationalism

Lukacs's analysis of philosophy follows a similar line of reasoning. As in the case of literature (Lukacs 1962), he traces the development of irrationalist tendencies within bourgeois thought. These are understood as arising from the sociohistorical conditions of class struggle:

> ... the first important period of modern irrationalism has its origin in the struggle against the idealist dialectical-historical concept of progress. It constitutes the road from the feudal reaction against the French Revolution to bourgeois hostility to progress (Lukacs 1981, 7).

Philosophically, class struggle is expressed, on the level of epistemology, in polemics against the idealist dialectic of Hegel in the period before 1848 and against historical materialism after 1848. In his view, Schelling, Schopenhauer, Kierkegaard and Nietzsche were the leading exponents of philosophical irrationalism in the 19th century.

For Lukacs, Schelling's philosophy represented a romantic reaction against science and the bourgeois conception of democracy. This was evident in Schelling's conception of intuition as the primary source of all knowledge and in his elitist notion of the inheritance of genius as an explanatory principle of philosophical development. In his later thought this tendency led directly to mysticism.

After the aborted revolution of 1848 philosophical irrationalism was exemplified and popularized in the writings of Schopenhauer, Kierkegaard and Nietzsche. In Schopenhauer and Kierkegaard irrationalism took the form of polemics against Hegelianism, the development of a pessimistic ontology of social isolation, and the denial of the very possibility of sociohistorical progress. In Nietzsche, whose philosophy Lukacs believed proved to be more influential as a precursor of fascism, irrationalism took the form of an anti-democratic ontology and the substitution of myth-making for historical analysis.

In the imperialist period between 1870 and World War I the leading philosophical tendency was that of vitalism. Lukacs considers Dilthey, Simmel, Spengler and Scheler as the main representatives of this philosophical trend in Germany. By vitalism, he means the substitution of a mythical conception of life for a concept of socio-historical existence. This philosophy led, in his view, to the false opposition between culture and civilization as the primary contradiction.

Philosophical polemics against democracy and socialism often took a highly abstract form. They opposed the very notion of human progress and the possibility of knowledge. Lukacs furnishes an outline of the basic irrationalist tendencies in modern philosophy from Schelling to Heidegger:

> The disparagement of understanding and reason, an uncritical glorification of intuition, an aristocratic epistemology, the rejection of sociohistorical progress, the creating of myths and so on are motives we can find in virtually any irrationalist (Lukacs 1981, 10).

It is important to understand that Lukacs's primary criticism of Heidegger is not against his famous speech in support of Hitler. It is instead against his ontology of the chaos of human existence expressed philosophically in *Being and Time*.

The political problem the analysis of irrationalism addresses is the rise of fascism. Lukacs's argument is that philosophical irrationalism provides the ideological grounds for fascism and that the despair implicit in irrationalism provides the social-psychological connection between the masses and the ideology of National Socialism. In his view, the racial theories of Chamberlain and Rosenberg are grounded in the irrationalist epistemology of vitalism. Rosenberg always spoke more about the "Jewish soul" than he did about any objective racial characteristics.

Lukacs's argument is not that Dilthey and Simmel were fascist ideologues, but rather that the epistemology of vitalism provides the irrationalist grounds for a racist theory of history. Rosenberg's theory is actually a synthesis of earlier racist theories with the subjectivist epistemology of vitalism and existentialism. Lukacs's analysis of irrationalism was written for western intellectuals. Although he argues that the irrationalist tendencies in philosophy were a response to the sociohistorical conditions of class struggle, it is clear to Lukacs that they were not the only possible response. In other words, his argument is that it is still possible for intellectuals to avoid lapsing into irrationalist epistemology through a philosophical commitment to the notion of human progress and the subject-object dialectic.

Lukacs vs. the Frankfurt School

The best known neo-Marxist analysis of the relationship between irrationalism and the rise of fascism is that of the Frankfurt School, particularly as expressed in the writings of Max Horkheimer and Theodor Adorno. *The Eclipse of Reason* by Horkheimer and *Dialectic of Enlightenment* by Horkheimer and Adorno are the most representative texts. Although Lukacs was familiar with the work of the Frankfurt School, he never developed a systematic critique of their point of view. It is safe to assert that he viewed the work of Horkheimer and Adorno as grounded in the irrationalist traditions of German philosophy.

The Destruction of Reason was published in 1955. Lukacs's aim was to articulate the struggle between irrationalist and rationalist tendencies in philosophy and social theory in the context of the cold war. In his view, many intellectuals were still operating with an irrationalist epistemology. This was true for both cold war liberals and neo-Marxist social theorists. Consider the following remark addressed to the intellectuals associated with the Frankfurt School:

> A considerable part of the leading German intelligentsia, including Adorno, have taken up residence in the "Grand Hotel Abyss" which I described in connection with my critique of Schopenhauer as a beautiful hotel, equipped with absurdity. And the daily contemplation of the abyss between excellent meals or artistic entertainments, can only heighten the enjoyment of the subtle comforts offered (Lukacs 1971b, 22).

This remark does not constitute a critique of epistemology. Here, Lukacs only asserts, through analogy, a connection between the Frankfurt School and the irrationalist epistemology and pessimism of the pre-fascist traditions in German philosophy. In Lukacs's view the Frankfurt School and their followers in the post-war period operated with what he referred to as "left ethics and right epistemology" (Lukacs 1971b, 21).

In other words, their commitment to human emancipation was grounded in a purely utopian conception of the role of theory. This position did not allow for the discussion of socialism in the real world. Their theory of domination was based on an essentialist myth of the identity between human and external nature. The connection Horkheimer and Adorno posit between the Enlightenment and the rise of fascism is dependent upon an abstract conception of the domination over nature as the principle of modern totalitarianism. This way of formulating the problem makes organized political struggle against capitalism irrelevant to the project of human emancipation. It leads to an attitude of passive resignation, despair, or elitism (Horkheimer and Adorno 1972).

Existentialism or Marxism

According to Lukacs, after World War II the most popular philosophical ideology was that of French existentialism. In 1948 he published his polemical essay, "Existentialism or Marxism?"(Lukacs 1964b). The thrust of his argument was directed against the epistemology and political implications of Sartre's *Being and Nothingness* (Sartre 1956). It was clear to Lukacs that there were fundamental differences of political perspective between the French existentialists and the pro-fascist stance of Heidegger. Maurice Merleau-Ponty, Simone de Beauvoir and Jean-Paul Sartre were ideologically anti-fascist and sympathetic to the Communist movement.

The critique of Sartre's philosophy was in terms of its epistemological grounding in the irrationalist traditions of European thought in the twentieth century. Lukacs criticized the conceptions of "nothingness" and "freedom," and their political implications in the context of the intensifying atmosphere of the cold war. There was something dangerous in the abstractness of Sartre's conception of freedom:

> Existentialism is the philosophy not only of death but also of abstract freedom. This is the most important reason for the popularity of Sartre's form of existentialism; and, although it may sound paradoxical, the reactionary side of existentialism's present influence is here concealed (Lukacs 1964, 147).

The double danger of this conception of freedom was that it could be used by the bourgeois reaction against the Communist movement and that it opened the door to the retreat into nihilism. In *The Destruction of*

Reason Lukacs had argued that cold war liberalism was as much based upon a nihilistic conception of life as was fascist ideology.

Lukacs's polemic against existentialism was not an attack against Sartre's conception of the role of individual choice and action in history, but rather against his nihilistic formulation of freedom. In *Search for a Method* (Sartre 1963) Sartre missed this point, arguing instead that the rejection of the individual had been the core of Lukacs's argument against him. But Lukacs's words are quite clear:

> What is the legitimate factor in Sartre? Without question, the emphasis on the individual's decision, whose importance was undervalued alike by bourgeois determinism and by vulgar Marxism. All social activity is made up of the actions of individuals, and no matter how decisive the economic basis may be in these decisions, its effects are felt only "in the long run," as Engels so often stresses (Lukacs 1964b, 150).

The problem is rather that Sartre denied the process of sociohistorical development and isolated the individual from his/her connection to society. The irony of his conception of freedom was that it results in a sense of fatalism. Like the modernist writers, he philosophically denied the possibility of human progress.

It should be kept in mind that Lukacs's polemic against existentialism was written before Sartre's attempted synthesis of existentialism and Marxism in *The Critique of Dialectical Reason* (Sartre 1976). It is unfortunate that Lukacs did not publish a critique of this latter work. It is clear from his writings that he was optimistic about Sartre's further intellectual development—an attitude he did not hold about either Horkheimer or Adorno.

Lukacs's Self Critique

In the 1960s Lukacs published new editions of *The Theory of the Novel* and *History and Class Consciousness*. Each book was accompanied by a new preface in which he discussed the intellectual and political context of their original publication. These prefaces also contained self-criticisms of his own epistemology and world-view during the period from 1917 to 1923. He criticized his own romanticism, utopianism and philosophical confusion from the point of view of his later critique of irrationalism. It should be kept in mind that in the 1960s, unlike in the late '20s and early '30s, when he published his repudiations of the "Blum Theses" and *History and Class Consciousness,* he was under no political pressure to offer a public rejection of his early writings.

In the preface to *The Theory of the Novel* Lukacs focused primarily on the intellectual influences and philosophical orientations underlying his analysis. He stressed the divergent influences of Dilthey, Simmel, Sorel and Max Weber upon his intellectual development and subjective radicalism. As he put it:

> *The Theory of the Novel is* not conservative but subversive in nature, even if based on a highly naive and totally unfounded Utopianism—the hope that a natural life worthy of man can spring from the disintegration of capitalism and the destruction, seen as identical with that disintegration of the lifeless and life-denying social and economic categories (Lukacs 1971b, 20).

In 1917 he had rejected capitalism in the name of a vitalist conception of "life." But now, in the 1960s, he uses the phrase "left ethics and right epistemology" in reference to his own philosophical position (Lukacs 1971b, 21).

In the preface to *History and Class Consciousness* Lukacs's central concern was with the idealist and utopian formulations of the problem of subjectivity. For example, he focused upon the mistaken way he had formulated the problem of alienation and the identical subject-object of history. Consider the following passages:

> For it is in Hegel that we first encounter alienation as the fundamental problem of the place of man in the world and vis-a-vis the world. However, in the term alienation he includes every type of objectification. Thus "alienation" when taken to its logical conclusion is identical with objectification.

> Thus the proletariat seen as the identical subject-object of the real history of mankind is no materialist consummation that overcomes the constructions of idealism. It is rather an attempt to out-Hegel Hegel, it is an edifice boldly erected above every possible reality and thus attempts objectively to surpass the Master himself (Lukacs 1971a, xxiii).

Lukacs's political concern was with the influence *The Theory of the Novel* and *History and Class Consciousness* had exercised upon neo-Marxist social theory in Western Europe, in particular upon the Frankfurt School and French existentialism. Here is how he expresses this concern:

If I have concentrated on my errors, there have been mainly practical reasons for it. It is a fact that *History and Class Consciousness* had a powerful effect on many readers and continues to do so even today. If it is the true arguments that achieve this impact, then all is well and the author's reaction is wholly uninteresting and irrelevant. Unfortunately I know it to be the case that, owing to the way society has developed and to the political theories this development has produced, it is precisely those parts of the book that I regard as theoretically false that have been the most influential (Lukacs 1971a, xxvii).

This is the reason for his caution and apprehension. He was concerned that his own writings might have provided the philosophical underpinning for the "left ethics and right epistemology" of Adorno, Sartre, and a younger generation of social theorists. This passage also draws attention to the general thesis of *The Destruction of Reason*—the role intellectuals played during the inter-war and postwar periods.

Conclusion

The most obvious criticism which can he made against Lukacs is that he idealizes reason and simplifies philosophical problems in order to judge most of modern philosophy and literature as irrational. This is the basis for Susan Sontag's claim that his analysis is vile, simplistic and crude (Sontag 1966, 82-92). He leaves himself open to this criticism by not clearly articulating his conception of reason, saying only that it is the belief in the possibility of knowledge and human progress, without clearly articulating the difference between his own conception of reason and that of the Enlightenment. This difference is implicit in his formulation of the dialectic of a qualitative historical transformation of both experience and reality.

His position is actually less dogmatic than critics like Sontag claim. I do not believe that he intended to suggest that sociohistorical progress is inevitable, nor did he wish to defend a positivist conception of science. His aim was to defend Marxism against bourgeois irrationalism and to assert the primacy of the subject-object dialectic in historical analysis.

His philosophical writings were an attempt to clarify questions of epistemology. If we consider Lukacs's literary criticism of the 1930s, it is easy to see that the problem of knowledge was central. He rejected both mechanistic materialism and idealism. His solution was that the interaction between subject and object constitutes the process of historical development.

Lukacs defended the reflection theory of knowledge while rejecting naturalism in favor of realism (Lukacs 1971a, xxxvii). The former, he said, produced a photographic image of social reality, and the latter portrayed the dynamic process of historical development. He argued that literary modernism annihilated any image of external reality. A similar claim was leveled against most of modern philosophy. Lukacs's faith in human progress and the future development of socialism was grounded in philosophical arguments concerning the nature of historical reality and the capacity for human understanding and action.

For Lukacs, the subject-object dialectic is a philosophical presupposition of the nature of social reality and a principle guiding social analysis, preventing tendencies toward either idealism or mechanistic materialism. His conceptions of progress, historical development, and the dialectic do not constitute a new philosophy. They are an important contribution to the clarification of the principles enunciated by Marx.

For Lukacs, the theoretical problem connecting political and philosophical questions is the "role" intellectuals play during a period of generalized crisis. This is a problem which was insufficiently dealt with by both the Frankfurt School and the French existentialists. It is of particular relevance today given the reemergence of irrationalism during the 1970s and '80s in neo-conservative and neo-liberal social thought. Lukacs's analysis may shed light on both the general characteristics of irrationalism and the political dangers associated with it.

REFERENCES

Arato, Andrew and Paul Breines. 1979. *The Young Lukacs and the Origin of Western Marxism.* New York: Continuum Books.

Deutscher, Isaac. 1971. *Marxism in Our Time.* Berkeley, California: Ramparts Press.

Horkheimer, Max. 1974. *Eclipse of Reason.* New York: Continuum Books.

Horkheimer, Max and Theodor Adorno. 1972. *Dialectic of Enlightenment.* New York: Continuum Books.

Jameson, Frederic. 1971. *Marxism and Form: Twentieth Century Dialectical Theories of Literature.* Princeton: Princeton University Press.

Jay, Martin. 1973. *The Dialectical Imagination.* Boston: Little, Brown.

Lukacs, Georg. 1962. *The Historical Novel.* London: Merlin Press.

_____. 1963. *The Meaning of Contemporary Realism.* London: Merlin Press.

_____. 1964a. *Essays on Thomas Mann.* London: Merlin Press..

_____. 1964b. "Existentialism or Marxism?" in George Novack, ed., *Existentialism Versus Marxism.* New York: Dell.

_____. 1969. *Solzhenitsyn*. Cambridge, Mass.: MIT Press.

_____. 1971a. *History and Class Consciousness*. Cambridge: MIT Press (first published in 1923).

_____. 1971b. *The Theory of the Novel*. Cambridge: MIT Press.

_____. 1972a. *Political Writings*. London: New Left Books.

_____. 1972b. *Studies in European Realism*. London: Merlin Press.

_____. 1975. *The Young Hegel*. Cambridge: MIT Press.

_____. 1981. *The Destruction of Reason*. Atlantic Highlands, N.J.: Humanities Press.

Merleau-Ponty, Maurice. 1973. *Adventures of the Dialectic*. Evanston, Ill: Northwestern University Press.

Poster, Mark. 1975. *Existential Marxism in Postwar France*. Princeton: Princeton Univesrity Press.

Sartre, Jean-Paul. 1956. *Being and Nothingness*. Secaucus, N.J: Citadel Press.

_____. 1963. *Search for a Method*. New York: Vintage Books.

_____. 1976. *The Critique of Dialectical Reason*. London: New Left Books.

Sontag, Susan. 1966. *Against Interpretation*. New York: Dell.

CHAPTER 3

Edward Said and the
Critique of Orientalism

Introduction

To readers unfamiliar with discourse analysis and the methods of literary criticism, *The Question of Palestine* by Edward Said may seem to be an odd sort of book. It first appears to be a political defense of the rights of the Palestinian people against Zionism and the policies of the Israeli state. The book, of course, is such a defense, but at the same time, it is also more than this.

Said begins his account of the history of Zionism with a discussion of George Eliot's last novel *Daniel Deronda,* published in 1876. He remarks:

> The unusual thing about the book is that its main subject is Zionism, although the novel's principal themes are recognizable to anyone who has read Eliot's earlier fiction. Seen in the context of Eliot's general interest in idealism and spiritual yearning, Zionism for her was one in a series of worldly projects for the nineteenth-century mind still committed to hopes for a secular religious community (Said 1979, 60-61).

It might seem more logical to have begun with a discussion of the Balfour Declaration of 1917, the writings of Theodore Herzl, or the actual European migration to Palestine from the 1880s to 1948. The plausible reason for beginning with George Eliot is the role European intellectuals have played in defining the way in which the Palestinians and the Zionists would be understood within Europe and the United States. The role each group would play was defined more by discourse and interpretation than by any immediately experienced reality.

Said's analysis of Zionism and of contemporary Western attitudes toward Islam and the entire Middle East is grounded in his analysis of the ideology of Orientalism. It is in this sense that his trilogy—*Orientalism, The Question of Palestine,* and *Covering Islam*—possesses a logical and historical coherence. These works attempt to disclose the ideological underpinnings of the very definition of the cultural distinction between Europe and the so-called Orient. This distinction is less a question of empirical fact than one of cultural definition and the power to define through textual representation. In *Orientalism* Said established the theoretical and historical premises for the analysis of the contemporary situation, and it is in this context that *The Question of Palestine* and *Covering Islam* are concrete applications of the general theory of Orientalism as a hegemonic ideology.

In this essay I will first discuss the main features of Edward Said's theory of Orientalism. My primary focus will be upon the way in which he has applied discourse analysis and the methods of literary criticism to the study of history, society, and the internal dynamics of political struggle. I will then discuss his conception of criticism and the role of the critic, which is a central component of this theory. I will pay particular attention in my own critique to the epistemological and ethical presuppositions underlying this analysis. I will argue that Said's political analysis expresses a commitment to the leading principles of the secular humanist tradition exemplified by the philosophy of Vico, and that his conception of criticism defines both the progressive nature and limits of his analysis.

The Critique of Orientalism

Edward Said's analysis of Orientalism is grounded in a theory of representation. Central to this analysis is the way in which meaning is constituted through discourse and interpretation. The actual facts play a minimal role in understanding the "real Orient" since the Orient is itself a feature of Western discourse which has established the cultural boundary between Orient and Occident.

In order to carry out this analysis, Said read and analyzed works by the leading academic Orientalists of the nineteenth and twentieth centuries such as Silvestre de Sacy, Ernest Renan, Edward William Lane, and H. A. R. Gibb. These academic writings were analyzed in terms of the political context of colonial domination by the French and English from Napoleon's conquest of Egypt in 1798 through World War II and the U.S. domination of the region which followed. It is in this context that academic Oriental-ism, imaginative writing, and the writings of imperial administrators are treated as constituting a discourse on and about the

Orient.

Said views his own analysis of Orientalism as being similar in form to the method of discourse analysis utilized by Michel Foucault in *Discipline and Punish.* The connection might also be drawn to the analysis of texts made by Raymond Williams in *The Country and the City.* The fundamental aim in each of these analyses is to establish the construction of a way of perceiving reality. In his own work, Said lays great stress upon the significance of individual authors since they serve as points of reference within the discourse of Orientalism:

> The unity of the large ensemble of texts I analyze is due in part to the
> fact that they frequently refer to each other: Orientalism is after all a
> system for citing works and authors (Said 1978, 23).

It seems that it is this feature of making reference to other writers which characterizes the specific nature of Orientalist discourse and which also imbues individual texts with a special importance.

For Said, Orientalism is a system of moral and epistemological order which became an institutionalized discourse representing knowledge of the Orient. The professional Orientalist mediates the relationship between the Orient and the Western consumer of his cultural productions. Orientalism is a style of thought which is based upon a fundamental ontological distinction between the Orient and the Occident. Imaginative writers like Honoré de Balzac, Gustave Flaubert, Victor Hugo, Sir Walter Scott, and George Eliot are noteworthy for their acceptance of this distinction as fact and for their depiction of the Orient in great works of Western fiction. Orientalism as a doctrine and as a way of understanding the world has become part of European and North American material and cultural reality. For Said, the ideology of Orientalism expresses a fundamental power relationship on the level of culture:

> In the first place, culture is used to designate not merely something to
> which one belongs but something that one possesses and, along with
> that proprietary process, culture also designates a boundary by which
> the concepts of what is extrinsic or intrinsic to the culture come into
> forceful play (Said 1983, 8-9).

It is through this form of cultural operation that the distinction between "we" and "they" is established. This feature of culture describes the history of Orientalism during the nineteenth and twentieth centuries. The difference between the Orientalist and the Oriental is that the former writes about the latter, while the latter assumes the role of passive Other.

Although Said traces the development of Orientalism from ancient Greece to the present, his primary concern is with the hegemonic role this ideology has played from the Napoleonic period to the present. Modern Orientalism involves a close interaction between political, economic, and cultural interests. It was during the nineteenth century that Orientalism was transformed from a scholarly discourse into an imperial institution. It is in the context of colonial expansion that the speeches and writings of colonial administrators like Evelyn Baring Cromer and Arthur Balfour become important elements of Orientalist discourse. Great works of literature, travel books, scholarly writings, and political speeches become the archival materials which share commonly held beliefs and values concerning the nature of the Orient.

As I remarked earlier, Orientalism had been dominated by French and British scholars and imaginative writers from the end of the eighteenth century through World War II. This period of French and British cultural hegemony closely followed European colonial conquest. Since World War II, the United States has replaced France and England in both its political domination of the Middle East and through the development of area studies concerning this region. U.S. Orientalism has been dominated by the application of social-scientific methodology and research with the exclusion of any emphasis upon literature. It would seem from Said's analysis that this stress upon "facts" has even further dehumanized our conception of the people of this region. Social science has reduced the population to attitudes, trends, and statistics. There is no longer the need for scholars to understand the language or cultural traditions of the region. A very powerful and well-funded support system exists for the promotion of Middle East area studies in the United States.

Edward Said attempts to develop a theory of cultural domination which is grounded in Gramsci's theory of hegemony. His own specific contribution to this theory relies upon the application of literary theory and discourse analysis to the sphere of cultural life. His study of Orientalism serves as a concrete example of how this analysis can be applied to a specific cultural domain and set of political problems. In principle, the analysis he develops in *Orientalism* could be equally applied to the field of Sovietology, Latin American studies, or women's studies. He has provided a useful model for further research and analysis of cultural domination of all sorts.

The strengths of his analysis also embody many of its own limitations.

For example, his treatment of modern Orientalism as a feature of colonialism lacks anything that might be called a theory of imperialism. It seems that he intentionally avoids the very possibility of situating his analysis within the framework of a theory of capitalism. Nevertheless, his historical account of modern Orientalism closely follows the process of European expansion and domination.

An additional problem is in the very conception of Orientalism as a totally hegemonic force. Said's analysis ends with a depiction of Orientalism as a kind of immutable all-encompassing ideology. In short, there seems to be little space for counterhegemonic struggle other than in the form of courageous individual scholars who resist out of moral revulsion. In his own view, Orientalism constitutes a set of inherited beliefs somewhat akin to a religious doctrine. This is what makes the struggle against Orientalism even more difficult than it might initially seem.

The solution offered by Said is based upon a humanist conception of the role of the intellectual in modern society. This role is conceived in universalist terms:

> Perhaps if we remember that the study of human experience usually has an ethical, to say nothing of a political, consequence in either the best or worst sense, we will not be indifferent to what we do as scholars. And what better norm for the scholar than human freedom and knowledge (Said 1978, 327)?

This position provides the logical connection between the analysis of Orientalism and that of Zionism.

Zionism and the Palestinians

The second volume of Edward Said's trilogy, *The Question of Palestine*, was written immediately after the signing of the Camp David accords. This book might be understood as an attempt by a Palestinian American to write the history of Zionism from the point of view of its victims. This is no simple task given the longstanding denial of any public space in U.S. civil society for the presentation of the history of the Palestinian people, and their political and human rights. As Said wrote in 1988: "It is as if even the narrative of Palestinian history is not tolerable, and therefore must be told and re-told innumerable times" (Said and Hitchens 1988, I i). Given this tradition of denial, the presentation of the narrative of the history of Palestine becomes an important political act.

As Said argues in *The Question of Palestine,* all appeals on behalf of

Zionism were international. The site of Zionist struggle was only partially in Palestine. Most of the time this struggle took place in Europe and in the United States, where propaganda and liberal discourse have played an important role in defining this political conflict. It is in this context that he stresses the role Western intellectuals have played in their representation of Israeli society and the Zionist project. He strongly criticizes the accounts by intellectuals like Reinhold Niebuhr, Edmund Wilson, Saul Bellow, and Gary Wills on the progressive features of Israeli society which maintain an attitude of silence about the treatment of the Palestinians—arguing that these writings are symptomatic of a bias which does not even acknowledge the humanity of the Palestinians.

Said suggests that during the nineteenth century the expert Orientalists were looked to for knowledge about the Orient. However, today we turn to Zionism for this knowledge. The attitudes and practices of British scholars, colonial administrators, and experts did much to prepare the way for the development of the contemporary attitude toward the Palestinians within Israel and the United States:

> Most of all, I think, there is the entrenched *cultural* attitude toward Palestinians deriving from age-old Western prejudices about Islam, the Arabs, and the Orient. This attitude, from which in its turn Zionism drew for its view of the Palestinians, dehumanized us, reduced us to the barely tolerated status of a nuisance (Said 1979, xiv).

He argues that between Zionism and the West there is a community of language and ideology. The Arabs are not part of this community; they are generally depicted as its enemy.

It has often been forgotten in the United States that while important European intellectuals were considering the fate of Palestine, the Palestinians believed that it was their homeland. For Said, the significance of the Balfour Declaration is that it took for granted the higher right of a colonial power to dispose of a territory as it saw fit: "There is not much use today in lamenting such a statement as the Balfour Declaration. It seems more valuable to see it as part of a history" (Said 1979, 16). The Balfour Declaration is an important part of the legacy of Orientalism and all of its stated and unstated cultural assumptions concerning the character of the native population of Palestine.

For most of its modern history the population of Palestine has been subject to denial. In order to deny the presence of natives on a desired land, the Zionists had to convince themselves and much of the rest of the world that the Palestinians did not exist as a people. It is in this context that the publication of Joan Peters's *From Time Immemorial* in 1984 was an attempt to provide ideological justification for denying all rights to the Palestinians. Her central claim is that significant numbers of Palestinians did not live in Palestine until the period 1946-48, when they migrated to take advantage of the economic development which resulted from Zionist enterprise. For Said, the lack of any critical response to her book in the United States clearly shows the low level of rational discourse within the liberal intellectual community (Said and Hitchens 1988, 23-31).

The fact is that Arabs have generally been represented in the Western media and seldom allowed to speak for themselves and present their point of view. There are few articles in the mass media or books published by Arabs; it seems that someone always has the role of speaking for them. This has led to the refusal to grant them any place in actuality. Said argues that Palestinians have not been given the opportunity to represent themselves and their history and that this process follows the general pattern established by Orientalism in the nineteenth century.

Said's discussion of Palestinian history and the conflict between Zionism and the Palestinians is not simply a narrative of events and circumstances. In his view:

> The question of Palestine is therefore the contest between an affirmation and a denial, and it is this prior contest, dating back over a hundred years, which animates and makes sense of the current impasse between the Arab states and Israel... But we need to try to understand what the instruments of this contest were, and how they shaped subsequent history so that this history now *appears* to confirm the validity of the Zionist claims to Palestine, thereby denigrating the Palestinian claims (Said 1979, 8).

He goes on to argue that the concealment of the real history of Zionism has become institutionalized in the Western media and intellectual discourse and that the open discussion of this history is a necessary feature of any comprehensive peace in the Middle East.

This history is one which has been heavily influenced by the weight of argument, interpretation, and selective silence. Edward Said's analysis of the tormented history of the Palestinian people and their struggle for self-determination is grounded in his analysis of the ideology of Orientalism and the practice of Western colonialism. His criticisms of Zionism and the practices of the Israeli state since 1948 are grounded in a theory of universal human rights:

> The long-run goal is, I think, the same for every human being, that
> politically he or she may he allowed to live free from fear, insecurity,
> terror, and oppression, free also from the possibility of exercising unequal
> or unjust domination over others (Said 1979, 53).

I do not believe that Said's articulation of the existence of fundamental
human rights such as self-determination is simply a tactical or rhetorical
gesture. The assumption of human rights for all people regardless of race,
religion, class, or gender is a feature of the secular humanist tradition,
which is the philosophical foundation for his literary studies and approach
to politics. This position rejects any double standard in relationship to the
issues of democracy, human rights, or terrorism. In this sense, his ethical
position is very similar to that of Noam Chomsky.

The United States and Iran

As in the case of *The Question of Palestine, Covering Islam* was written
as a political intervention. Said's central focus was on the way Islam was
being presented in the United States during the Iranian hostage crisis. He
viewed the coverage of this crisis as reflecting the well-established
traditions of Orientalism and the political pressures of the immediate
situation. The term "covering" had a double meaning, referring to both
the "reporting of" and "covering over" the realities and complexities of
Islamic society.

In this study, Said focuses more upon the role of the mass media than
academic Orientalism or the texts of high culture. For example, he
mentions the fact that during the first days of the hostage crisis there were
three hundred reporters in Teheran, none of whom read Persian. Most of
the reports that came out of Iran stressed the character of the Islamic
mind and anti-U.S. feelings, while more complex human realities were
either ignored or denied.

He argues that the mass media give consumers of news the sense that
they have an understanding of Islam:

> In many instances "Islam" has licensed not only patent inaccuracy but
> also expressions of unrestrained ethnocentrism, cultural and even racial
> hatred, deep yet paradoxically free-floating hostility (Said 1981, xi).

It must be kept in mind that the current images of Islamic society are
reinforced by the entire tradition of Orientalist scholarship and literary

representations of the Orient. Authorities are readily cited to substantiate the idea that Islam is medieval and a danger to Western civilization.

Said states that the aim of his book is not to provide a defense of Islamic society, but instead to analyze the uses of "Islam" in the West. He is aware that his method of textual analysis does not allow him to affirm the viability of Iranian or other Islamic societies. It is more useful as a way of pointing out distortions or misrepresentations than it is in providing an authentic image of sociohistorical reality.

From his analysis we can see quite readily the absurdity of the statements and images of Islam which are routinely presented in the mass media. We can recognize their absurdity since we know that similar kinds of generalizations could not be made about Europe or Catholicism. For example, prejudicial statements about "Catholic society" or the "European mind" would not even make sense. It is only possible to say such things about a distant Other.

The paradox in the representation of Islam is that its alterity often takes on the appearance of a simple immediacy: "There is an unstated assumption, first of all, that the proper name 'Islam' denotes a simple thing to which one can refer immediately" (Said 1981, 38). Accompanying this immediacy is the tendency to treat Islam as something without a history of its own. In the present context it is reduced to being in a conflictual relationship with the West over oil or hostages. In reality, Islam has had a rich history and a diverse societal existence. The mass media have reduced this complexity to a flattened reality. While the West is presented as modern secular society, Islam is presented as being stuck in religious primitivism and backwardness.

One of the significant theoretical formulations in *Covering Islam* is Said's conception of "communities of interest" and the problem of interpretation:

> What we are dealing with here are in the very widest sense communities of interpretation, many of them at odds with one another, prepared in many instances literally to go to war with one another, all of them creating and revealing themselves and their interpretations as very central features of their existence (Said 1981, 41).

In this context he attempts to deal with the relationship between the political power and economic interests that underlie representations of individuals, groups, and societies. He argues that all knowledge concerning human society is historical. This knowledge rests upon both moral judgments and the interpretation of what are taken to be the key facts. These interpretations depend upon who the interpreters are, whom they are addressing, what purposes are at stake, and at what moment in human history the interpretations are taking place: "It is related to what other interpreters have said, either by confirming them, or by disputing them, or by continuing them" (Said 1981, 154).

Said's main point here is that no interpretation can be complete without an examination of the situation of the interpreter:

> Every interpreter is a reader, and there is no such thing as a neutral or value-free reader. Every reader, in other words, is both a private ego and a member of a society with affiliations of every sort linking him or her to that society (Said 1981, 156).

In this view, every reader is situated and constrained by his or her education, the prevailing ideological currents, material interests, and institutional power.

After having established the problem of power and interest underlying every interpretation, Said then turns to a subjective way out of this dilemma by asserting the freedom of choice that every intellectual makes:

> whether to put intellect at the service of power or at the service of criticism, community, and moral sense. This choice must be the first act of interpretation today, and it must result in a decision, not simply a postponement (Said 1981, 164).

Earlier on he had remarked: "By using the skills of a good critical reader to disentangle sense from nonsense, by asking the right questions and expecting pertinent answers, anyone can learn about either 'Islam' or the world of Islam" (Said 1981, xix). This assertion of individual choice would seem to negate the entire problem of interpretation if it could be exercised in such a willful manner. This position seems to suggest that all readers need do is make the correct moral commitment and then proceed free from the interests that otherwise have the capacity to distort all interpretation. This apparent paradox leads directly to the examination of Said's conception of criticism and the role of the critic in society.

The problem is not that there may not be a real basis for a counterhegemonic movement within civil society. The problem with Said's formulation of this possibility is that it is too abstract and individualistic. The choice that the critic makes is itself outside of any real historical context. After having established a theory of hegemony well grounded in history, he then seems to set this aside in the name of an abstract freedom.

Criticism and the World

In 1983 Edward Said published a collection of essays under the title *The World, the Text, and the Critic.* Although these essays cover a wide range of topics (from Orientalism to recent developments in literary theory), the main focus of his concern is identifying the role of the critic in contemporary society. Most of the essays go beyond the field of literary criticism as it is narrowly defined. Much of the book expresses a strong polemic against "deconstructionism" and the influence of Jacques Derrida upon the development of criticism in the United States.

Said argues that the dominant currents in literary theory have led to a fetishism of the text and the denial of historical reality in the name of methodological rigor:

> Even if we accept (as in the main I do) the arguments put forward by Hayden White—that there is no way to get past texts in order to apprehend "real" history directly—it is still possible to say that such a claim need not also eliminate interest in the events and the circumstances entailed by and expressed in the texts themselves (Said 1983, 4).

In his view, texts are themselves events grounded in sociohistorical reality. He takes the ontological position that texts are part of the social world and the historical moment in which they are written and read. This position assumes the objective existence of a social world which is knowable through representation. His own views concerning the ontological status of reality are similar to those of Georg Lukacs and Raymond Williams and are in direct opposition to the main currents of contemporary literary criticism.

He also argues that the texts of high culture should occupy no privileged position for critics. Criticism should not assume that its domain is merely the literary text. It should see its project of criticism and interpretation in terms of a more general, and in principle, more democratic conception of discourse. What matters is the continuity and transformation of knowledge and experience through cultural signification. This point of view rejects the elitist traditions of literary criticism without abandoning the critical project of reading and interpretation. In fact, it assumes that the trained critic has an important role to play within civil society.

Said argues that no reading of the text is neutral; every text and every reading is, in his view, the product of a "theoretical stance." Although critics may often deny this simple fact, in doing so they risk becoming irrelevant to the ethical and political life of society:

> In having given up the world entirely for the aporias and unthinkable paradoxes of a text, contemporary criticism has retreated from its constituency, the citizens of modern society. who have been left to the hands of "free" market forces, multinational corporations, the manipulations of consumer appetites (Said 1983, 4).

This position assumes that the critic can make an important contribution to the liberation of society from a diverse range of tyrannical and oppressive forces. However, in order for contemporary critics to begin playing this role, they must first give up much of their elitism and their definition of criticism "as the endless misreading of a misinterpretation" (Said 1983, 25).

Said assumes that there exists potential for active resistance within civil society and that much of contemporary criticism has lost contact with this reality. In his view, the roads taken by much of contemporary criticism (including left criticism) result from a theoretical and epistemological stance and an active will. Although the power of material interests and hegemonic ideology is great, it is presumed that individual critics have chosen deconstructionism as their central paradigm and that they can reject this for a theory of criticism grounded in radical humanism. The unexamined problem is the relationship between the critic and social movements for liberation.

At stake here is the relationship between intellectuals and political parties and other mass organizations. But what is also crucial is the theoretical conception of society as a "collectivity" or as a "collection of individuals" mediated by institutions, practices, and discourse. Said often seems to prefer the latter to the former, and as a consequence, ends up with a highly individualistic conception of choice, responsibility, and action. His theory of criticism lacks an adequate conception of agency which would transcend the notion of a purely individual ethical choice. After having established "the critic" as the unique individual, he is then faced with the problem of reintegrating the role of critic into a civil society defined by conflict, resistance, and accommodation to the existing order.

Even when Said formulates society as a collectivity possessing a history, he still conceives of the critic as an individual consciousness located on the margins of society. This relationship is one of permanent alienation. It is from this vantage point that the critic produces critical consciousness for civil society:

> For in the main—and here I shall be explicit—criticism must think of itself as life-enhancing and constitutively opposed to every form of tyranny, domination, and abuse; its social goals are non-coercive knowledge produced in the interests of human freedom (Said 1983, 29).

Needless to say this is hardly a historical conception of criticism. The world and the critic are viewed as being in a state of permanent opposition. As an alternative to recent trends in literary theory, Said formulates an untheorized conception of criticism as "critical consciousness." In his view, critical consciousness represents the awareness of different social situations; it is also the awareness that no system or theory exhausts human reality. He goes as far as setting up a fundamental opposition between theory and criticism:

> Indeed I would go as far as saying that it is the critic's job to provide resistances to theory, to open it up toward historical reality, toward society, toward human needs and interests, to point up those concrete instances drawn from everyday reality that lie outside or just beyond the interpretive area necessarily designated in advance and thereafter circumscribed by every theory (Said 1983, 242).

The problem with this formulation is that it is not clear what could possibly be meant by "historical reality," "society," "human needs and interests," and "everyday reality" since each of these is a concept and could only be understood as a feature of a theory of history and society.

The opposition between criticism and theory is dependent upon ontological claims concerning a reality beyond the purview and interpretive area of theory. How Said has come to the assertion of the primacy of the real as opposed to the limits of theoretical understanding is never made clear. This primacy is simply given as constituting the necessary conditions for the critical enterprise of demystification and as the grounds for resisting all forms of domination and tyranny. Having rejected deconstructionism as a nihilistic philosophy, he then opposes the idea of a master discourse or totalizing theory by means of ontological assertions of an extra-theoretical reality which is knowable through the act of criticism.

Religious and Secular Criticism

In the conclusion of *The World, the Text and the Critic,* Said returns to the problem of Orientalism in the context of a discussion of religious and secular criticism. In reference to the idea of the Orient, he remarks:

> To say of such grand ideas and their discourse that they have something in common with religious discourse is to say that each serves as an agent of closure, shutting off human investigation, criticism, and effort in deference to the authority of the more-than-human, the supernatural, the other-worldly (Said 1983, 290).

The key term in this passage is the idea of "closure." Religious ideas act as an inhibition upon the development of secular criticism. They offer the authority of the sacred and silence the possibility of reason and a critical attitude.

Said draws the analogy between religious discourse and the traditions of Orientalism. These sets of ideas are linked by their generality and presumption of authority. In turn, he goes on to suggest that a series of terms in contemporary political discourse suffer from a similar fate:

> As I have said, impossibly huge generalizations like the Orient, Islam, Communism, or Terrorism play a significantly increased role in the contemporary Manichean theologizing of "the Other," and this increase is a sign of how strongly religious discourse has affected discourse pertaining to the secular, historical world (Said 1983, 291).

In the present context, terms like "communism" and "terrorism" do not make reference to a distinctive human reality or practice, but rather establish a demonology of good and evil. Since these terms are grandiose, rather than finite, rational analysis and argument are excluded as human possibilities.

Said's alternative to religious discourse is the development of a truly secular criticism. His model for the distinction between religious and secular criticism is the distinction made by Vico between secular and sacred history:

> There is a great difference between what in *The New Science* Vico described as the complex, heterogeneous, and "gentile" world of nations and what in contrast he designated as the domain of sacred history. The essence of that difference is that the former comes into being, develops in various directions, moves toward a number of culminations, collapses, and then begins again—all in ways that can be investigated because

historians, or new scientists, are human and can know history on the
grounds that it was made by men and women (Said 1983, 290-91).

Since sacred history is made by God, it is beyond human understanding.
The philosophical grounds for Said's conception of secular criticism are
to be found in Vico and the tradition of secular humanism which has
developed since the publication of *The New Science.*

Said's affinity for Vico's formulation of the problem of language and
knowledge is clearly stated in the final chapter of *Beginnings: Intention
and Method* (Said 1976, chapter 6), where he opposes Vico's conception
of humanism to the perspectives of structuralism and poststructuralism.
His own conception of criticism embodies recent developments in
discourse analysis and a traditional humanist conception of the knowing
subject. It is on the basis of this formulation that he criticizes recent
developments in literary theory as expressive of a new irrationalism and
mysticism.

In *Beginnings: Intention and Method,* he was more generous in his
evaluation of the innovations in literary criticism achieved by structuralism
than he was later to become in *The World, the Text, and the Critic,* where
he polemicized against the variants of deconstructionism.

In Said's view, deconstructionism represents the revival of religious
criticism in a new form. Unlike the discourse of Orientalism, which seeks
closure, deconstructionism promotes mysticism, the fundamental
unintelligibility of language, and a withdrawal from political engagement.
As a consequence, the critic becomes either mute or simply irrelevant to
the political life of his or her society. It is in this context that Said offers
the alternative of a secular humanist conception of criticism.

Marxism and the Critique of Orientalism

Although most Marxists can easily support the political project of Said's
critique of Orientalism, few have taken his work seriously enough to offer
a critical commentary upon it. One clear exception to this rule is the
Egyptian Marxist, Samir Amin. In his most recent book, *Eurocentrism,*
Amin discusses the critique of Orientalism in the context of his theory of
world capitalism.

Amin argues that Said's critique of Orientalism has the defect of not
having gone far enough in some respects and having gone too far in others.
He argues that Said has not gone far enough to the extent that he is satisfied
with denouncing Eurocentric prejudice without proposing a theoretical
explanation of Orientalism, and that he has gone too far in suggesting

that the ideology of Orientalism was already in existence in the Middle Ages. For Amin, Orientalism did not begin until the Renaissance. As he puts it: "Once it became capitalist and developed the power to conquer, Europe granted itself the right to represent others—notably `the Orient'— and even to judge them" (Amin 1989, 101). This is a power Europe did not always possess.

Amin attempts to situate the critique of Orientalism within his theory of capitalist development. He argues that prior to the sixteenth century, Europe occupied a peripheral status in relation to the dominance of the tributary mode of production in the Arab world. With the rise of capitalism in Europe, Eurocentrism and Orientalism assumed the role of dominant ideologies in the new world order. These systems of belief expressed the new power relations defined by the capitalist world economy. For Amin, prejudice against the Orient prior to the sixteenth century was more an expression of provincialism than Orientalism: "Dante relegated Mohammed to Hell, but this was not a sign of a Eurocentric conception of the world, contrary to what Edward Said has suggested. It is only a case of banal provincialism, which is something quite different, because it is symmetrical in the minds of the two opposing parties (Amin 1989, 74)." Amin's discussion of the relationship between Europe and the Arab world from antiquity to the Renaissance relies heavily upon the historical research of the French Marxist, Maxime Rodinson.

Amin does not make any substantive criticisms of Said's theory of representation, his analysis of texts, or his conception of criticism. Instead, he focuses upon the periodization of Orientalism and situates this ideology within the history of capitalism. Although Said's historical analysis of the relation between Europe and the Arab world deals primarily with the period from Napoleon's invasion of Egypt to the present, he also suggests that the roots of Orientalism can be traced back to antiquity. The project of *Eurocentrism* is to argue for a universal theory of history within the framework of Marxism. Said's own universalism is grounded in the humanist tradition as expressed in texts from Vico to Gramsci.

Conclusion
In my own view, Edward Said's analysis of the problem of Orientalism has made an important contribution to our general understanding of the role racism plays in political discourse. Given the context of the dominance of Eurocentrism in U.S. political life, Said's position has been a courageous one. This is not to suggest that many anti-Arab intellectuals have been swayed by the cogency of his analysis or his commitment to universal

standards of moral judgment. This would be to expect too much from a critical intervention. It might be argued that he has made an open hatred of the Arab or Islamic world more difficult to sustain without embarrassment or the minimum of self-criticism.

Said's analysis of Orientalism is grounded in a theory of representation. The reality of the distinction between Orient and Occident is less a question of historical fact than one of cultural distinction and definition. His analysis of discourse refers the reader to the problem of representation and misrepresentation. This way of formulating the problem might suggest that a true representation exists as an alternative to the actuality of misrepresentation. The theoretical problem underlying the analysis of the hegemonic ideology of Orientalism is not resolved by suggesting that a people or a society could be referred to in some immediate and essential way.

In practical terms Said would claim that better representations of the Other are both possible and politically desirable. It is in this context that he criticizes the misrepresentations of Islam, the Arabs, and the Palestinians. It is also in this context that his book *After the Last Sky* (1986) is an attempt to provide a narrative of the experience of the Palestinian people since the creation of the state of Israel in 1948. His account of Palestinian life attempts to represent the experience of oppression, displacement, and resistance from the perspective of a Palestinian intellectual. This narrative must be understood in terms of its opposition to the more totalizing discourse which excludes the Palestinian voice entirely. Although his narrative makes use of Jean Mohr's photography of Palestinian life, in addition to a textual representation, the aim is not to present a flattened reality, but rather to describe the diversity of experience and to provide a sense of a people possessing a history.

This type of narrative is an important intervention within a highly contested political discourse concerning rights, obligations, struggle, and human suffering. However, it does not resolve the theoretical questions raised by Said's conception of discourse and representation. These questions require some further investigation and reflection on the uses of language and the power relations which define the very context of representation.

Rather than a better representation of the Other, the most desirable situation would be one where the very category of otherness had been transcended both in thought and in social being. However, this is merely to suggest a desired state which has no immediate possibility of being realized. In the meantime, it makes perfect sense to struggle for better representations, not only in texts, but in movements, organizations, and the fabric of daily life. There is a real political relevance to being sensitized to the power of language to define and limit.

My suggestion that there is no power relationship between self and other should not be misunderstood as a call for the end of all distinction. Said seems to be aware of this very problem. It is not distinctions as such, but only those which seek to deny the essential humanity of individuals, groups, and entire societies which present political and theoretical problems. It is in this context that Said's rejection of the postmodernist notion of the death of the subject must be understood. This position represents his commitment to humanism and the possibility of creating a democratic and secular discourse linked to an emancipatory human project.

Like Foucault, Said stresses the centrality of power relations in his analysis of discourse. Texts are situated objects within a worldly discourse. They constitute meaning and define the limits of thought and action. His criticism of Foucault's conception of power is that it is too general and does not allow for resistance to total domination.

For Said the point of analyzing the political role of discourse is to identify a domain for struggle and resistance. His working through the massive quantity and density of representations of the "Orient" is part of an intellectual and political project. The philosophical presuppositions of this analysis are that since the hegemony achieved through the discourse of Orientalism is a human production, it is both knowable and in principle something which can be resisted and overcome. Many of the problems in his conception of criticism are tied to a search for a political alternative.

Since there exists no immediate translation of his theoretical critique into a political practice which could directly confront the hegemony of Orientalism, Said turns to an overly subjective and individualist conception of criticism. This turning inward toward critical consciousness as a political solution may be largely a response to a despair over the lack of a viable social movement in the United States which could link the plight of the Palestinians with anti-imperialist struggles in southern Africa and Central America. Solidarity and anti-interventionist movements have yet to come to full realization that the situation of the Palestinians is conjoined to other struggles for self-determination. This political reality has in no sense led Said into passive submission, but has instead forced him into a reliance upon what Gramsci once called "the optimism of the will."

There can be no such thing as a purely theoretical or individual solution to political problems. My point here is not to deny the importance of intellectual work, but rather to situate it in relation to the problems of concrete political struggle. Bringing about fundamental change in power relations, in the organization of society, and in the way in which meaning is constituted discursively can never simply result from willful action. Edward Said's conception of humanism and secular criticism has directed us toward the problem of hegemony and domination, but it does not provide a theoretical solution to this problem since he has been unable to imagine theoretically what role criticism can actually play within a highly dominated civil society. The perspective of criticism and critical consciousness cannot take us beyond the image of the enlightened but isolated intellectual.

In an article entitled "Opponents, Audiences, Constituencies and Community" (1982), Said seems to turn from a focus upon the critic and the role of criticism in society to that of the secular intellectual. A similar concern is expressed in a recent interview (1988). In his 1982 essay, Said criticizes the rigid disciplinary boundaries of literary criticism and the isolation of the critic from the larger political discourse of civil society. He suggests that the professional skills of the trained critic might be more fruitfully applied to the discourse of politics rather than the texts of high culture which define the guild profession of literary criticism. In addition, he suggests that what is really at stake in contemporary political debate is the reproduction of the hegemonic discourse or the intentional interference by intellectuals with the project of cultural domination. It is at this point that literary critics and other scholars can make an important intervention within the present reactionary political situation.

Although the turn from the conception of critic to that of secular intellectual does not avoid the problem of specifying choice and the context for political commitment, it does allow Said to move away from the conception of critical consciousness. Secular intellectuals are not isolated individuals possessing critical consciousness, but rather actors within a historical context and organically linked to audiences, constituencies, and opponents. It is at this point in the argument that Said returns to Gramsci and the problem of counter-hegemonic struggle. The contribution that trained critics can make involves the analysis of representation through a focus upon the uses of language and the constitution of discourse.

REFERENCES

Amin, Samir. 1989. *Eurocentrism.* New York: Monthly Review Press.

Chomsky, Noam. 1983. *The Fateful Triangle.* Boston: South End Press.

Foucault, Michel. 1977. *Discipline and Punish.* New York: Pantheon.

Lukacs, Georg. 1963. *The Meaning of Contemporary Realism.* London: Merlin Press.

Peters, Joan. 1985. *From Time Immemorial.* New York: Harper and Row.

Rodinson, Maxime. 1987. *Europe and the Mystique of Islam.* Seattle: Univ. of Washington Press.

Said, Edward W. 1976. *Beginnings: Intention and Method.* New York: Columbia Univ. Press.

_____. 1978. *Orientalism.* New York: Vintage Books.

_____. 1979. *The Question of Palestine.* New York: Vintage Books.

_____. 1981. *Covering Islam.* New York: Pantheon.

_____. 1982. "Opponents, Audiences, Constituencies and Community," *Critical Inquiry* 9 (Sept. 1982).

_____. 1983. *The World, the Text, and the Critic.* Cambridge: Harvard Univ. Press.

_____. 1986. *After the Last Sky.* New York: Pantheon.

_____. 1988. "American Intellectuals and Middle East Politics," *Social Text* 19/20 (Fall 1988).

Said, Edward W., and Christopher Hitchens, eds. 1988. *Blaming the Victims.* London and New York: Verso.

Vico, Giambattista. 1984. *The New Science of Giambattista Vico.* Ithaca: Cornell Univ. Press.

Williams, Raymond. 1973. *The Country and the City.* New York: Oxford Univ. Press.

CHAPTER 4

Between Humanism and Social Theory: The Cultural Criticism of Raymond Williams

The literary and cultural criticism of Raymond Williams occupies the discursive space between humanism and social theory. Williams's humanism is the untheorized articulation of cultural production and human agency. His analysis of meaning, cultural practices, and social institutions is carried out without either a theory of epistemology or historical transformation.

Williams's analysis of ideology is based upon a conception of philosophical realism, much like that of Edward Said and Georg Lukacs. His analysis of ideology in *The Country and the City* is based upon a distinction between real history and the distorted images of rural and urban life. Said's critique of Orientalism is based upon a similar distinction between images of the Orient and the real sociohistorical development of the Middle East.

Lukacs provided the epistemological grounds for the theory of realism. For him, realist writers like Thomas Mann provide a reflection of the objective conditions of social life through the representation of typical characters and the narration of plot. Novels written in the realist tradition display the subject/object dialectic of historical materialism. Their representation of social reality is implicitly grounded in a theory of history.

Raymond Williams's cultural criticism presupposes a relationship between the critic and the world without specifying this relationship in theoretical terms. Interpreting texts and cultural practices presupposes engagement with the pressing problems of theory and ideology. Ideological struggle is embodied in the relationship between knowledge and power throughout society. Williams practiced the craft of practical criticism. He read and interpreted texts and reflected upon changes in the lexical field and in social institutions His approach to cultural studies was grounded in a personal commitment to socialism and democracy. His commitment to socialism was grounded in ties to working-class communities and organizations.

Williams lacked an interest in the kinds of philosophical problems that occupied Lukacs, Adorno, and Althusser. He operated with a rather naive conception of human agency and historical change and wrote as if all that were necessary was the right kind of values and moral commitment. His only real contribution to Marxist social theory was a refinement of Gramsci's conception of hegemony. However, he did not even apply his concepts of dominant, emergent, and residual culture in his own political writings of the 1970s and '80s. Instead, he offered a reflection upon the politics of hope.

Culture and Politics

In *Culture and Society*, Williams traced the changing meaning of five words—industry, democracy, class, art, and culture—in English social thought during the nineteenth and twentieth centuries. It is clear from his account that he viewed culture as the dominant term, if only because it had become central to both literary criticism and social science (Williams 1976, 10 and 1979, 97). But it was central in different ways for these disciplines. The former was often openly elitist and conservative, while the latter was at least formally democratic and liberal.

Williams began working on *Culture and Society* in 1947. His primary motive was to oppose what he saw as a conservative appropriation of the idea of culture. His aim was to refute the uses of the term culture against democracy, socialists, the working class, and popular education (Williams 1979, 97-98). His foreword to *Culture and Society* states:

> The organizing principle of this book is the discovery that the idea of culture, and the word itself in its general modern uses, came into English thinking in the period which we commonly describe as that of the Industrial Revolution. The book is an attempt to show how and why this happened, and to follow the idea through to our own day (Williams 1983a, vii).

The polemical thrust of the book was against the conservative interpretation of the idea of culture in English social thought from Matthew Arnold to F. R. Leavis and T. S. Eliot. The postwar political environment of Britain provided the context not only for *Culture and Society* but for *The Long Revolution* and *The Country and the City*. In each of these studies, Williams's central concern was to examine the English tradition of social thought, with which he viewed his own work as constituting a dialogue.

Williams seems to have felt no need to carry on a debate with Marxist cultural theory until the 1970s. He had not read Lukacs or the Frankfurt School until the late 1960s. His two most important works of the '70s, *Marxism and Literature* and *Problems in Materialism and Culture*, were attempts to come to terms with both Marxism and his own previous analysis of culture. It is in the essays contained in these two volumes that he addressed theoretical questions concerning cultural analysis for the first time. The three volumes of essays published after his death (Williams 1989a, 1989b, and 1989c) are of general interest but contain no new contributions to cultural theory.

Toward the Idea of Society

"Society" is the one term whose analysis was absent from *Culture and Society*. The idea was hinted at and presupposed in the analysis of industry, democracy, class, art, and culture. However, Williams made no actual study of the emergence and meaning of society within nineteenth- or twentieth-century social thought. The closest he came to a discussion of the use of the term was when he analyzed Thomas Carlyle's response to the industrial factory system and the cash nexus (Williams 1983a, chapter 4).

Williams devoted a chapter of *The Long Revolution* to the discussion of images of society without making reference to specific authors or sources. This was a general reflection upon the meanings embodied in a series of ideas or conceptions of society. The subjects of the images he discussed included the royal family, organic society, the nation-state, market society, human brotherhood, class conflict, and mass society. Each image defined the social purpose and the role of individuals within a collectivity (Williams 1961, part I, chapter 4).

Williams did not utilize the same method of analysis in *The Long Revolution* that he used in *Culture and Society*. His reflections upon the meanings of dominant ideas were much more general and not grounded in close readings of texts. Based on these reflections, he attempted to develop a social theory that would be capable of providing an adequate understanding of both society and historical change.

His theoretical conception of society consisted of four interrelated "systems": politics, culture, economics, and family (Williams 1961, 116).

Despite the plausibility of this list, the nature of the interrelations was never clearly articulated, leaving readers with an untheorized multiplicity of formations. He rejected economic determinism as an adequate explanation of historical change and moved, as if compelled by empirical findings, to concrete analyses of education, general literacy, the rise of a reading public, and the popular press.

Williams's entry for "society" in *Keywords* made particular reference to the relationship between society as a "generalization" and as an "abstraction":

Society is now clear in two main senses: as our most general term for the body of institutions and relationships within which a relatively large group of people live: and as our most abstract term for the condition in which such institutions and relationships are formed (Williams 1976, 243).

His particular interest was in articulating the difficult relationship between these two meanings of society as these senses of the word emerged in nineteenth- and twentieth-century use. For Williams, "society" referred both to an aspect of the process of historical development in the context of industrialization and urbanization and to the resulting interdependence and institutional framework of collective life.

In *The English Novel* and *The Country and the City*, Williams approached the idea of society from a quite different vantage point. Although his discussion was not systematic, he nevertheless began to address the emergence of the idea in the nineteenth-century English novel. His analysis began with a conception of the "knowable community." As he put it in both *The English Novel* and *The Country and the City*:

Most novels are in some sense knowable communities. It is part of a traditional method - an underlying stance and approach - that the novelist offers to show people and their relationships in essentially knowable and communicable ways (Williams 1970, 14 and 1973, 165).

But at a certain point in historical development the "knowable community" no longer adequately depicts the reality of social experience. Williams understood capitalist industrialization and urbanization as the key factors in the process of this change:

We can see its obvious relation to the very rapidly increasing size and scale and complexity of communities: in the growth of towns and especially of cities and of a metropolis, in the increasing division and complexity of labor; in the altered and critical relations between and within social classes (Williams 1970, 16).

In his view these developments had led to a crisis in the understanding of social relations. The "knowable community" could, from that point on, only be understood as a fragment of a larger and unknowable social whole. While the "knowable community" could still depict the local reality of social experience, the idea of society could only refer to an abstract conception of social being. Society became a question of scale and complexity, a term of analysis whose referent would always be in question.

While Williams's concept of society is insightful in this regard, it is inadequate as a foundation for a social theory. This was more the case for *Culture and Society* and *The Long Revolution* than for *The English Novel* and *The Country and the City*. In *Culture and Society* and *The Long Revolution*, his conception of "society" referred to a system of cultural values that was commonly shared by the citizens of a nation-state. Society was, then, an accident of territory. He came closer to a sociologically useful formulation of the concept of society as a form of life in his later works, particularly in *The Country and the City* and in his theoretical essays of the 1970s. For this, his early discussion of culture would prove important.

Literature and Ideology

In an interview with the editors of *New Left Review*, Williams remarked that the starting point for the analysis presented in *The Country and the City* was the English country-house poems (Williams 1979, 303). In this choice of subject matter he was responding to a literary orthodoxy that had provided much of the ideological basis for the organic image of rural society in English social thought. His analysis began with the way these pastoral poems were typically read within the field of literary studies. He then attempted to demystify the image of the country house and to provide a historical grounding for the relationship of this literary image of order to a disorderly world of labor and exploitation.

At the same time that Williams was addressing ideological aspects of literary studies, he was attempting to come to terms with the more general significance of the image of the countryside in English social thought. His premise was that the contrast between the country and the city had become an important focus of social experience in the nineteenth and twentieth centuries, and that this contrast is not only one of ideas and experience but also one "of rent and interest, of situation and power" (Williams 1973, 7). *The Country and the City* is Williams's most overtly Marxist study in that he directly linked cultural representations with the social relations of production. It is a study in ideology and power, grounded in the political economy of capitalism.

Williams read and analyzed a diverse range of writings including novels, plays, essays, and autobiographies. He did not provide a methodological discussion as to how these writings differ and how to go about interpreting texts. Instead of systematic interpretation we are given the craft of the literary critic and his sensitivity to nuance, tone, and characterization. Within this analysis, there is a clearly articulated tension between what might be called "historical fact" and "perspective."

Williams treated the writers whose works he analyzed as witnesses. Their writings were dealt with in terms of perception and the representation of meaning. The central issue concerning these writings was not historical error but historical perspective (Williams 1973, 10). The distinction between two levels of reality, fact and interpretation, play an important role in the history disclosed by *The Country and the City*.

Williams actually dealt with two different kinds of writings in his analysis. The first were literary and were read in terms of the perspective they reflected, which required interpretation and grounding within the history of capitalism. The second were historical studies which Williams read as factual evidence rather than for their interpretation of events. His analysis assumes that historical writing can provide much of the factual basis for situating literary representations. Numerous histories were relied upon in his discussion of processes like enclosure or the economic development of particular cities. These writings were neither directly cited nor treated as if they also required critical analysis. Instead, they were treated as providing factual evidence for judgments concerning representation and misrepresentation.

A conception of philosophical realism underlies Williams's approach to the presence of ideology within literary texts. For example, he argued that the country was often idealized as a natural and moral economy in opposition to the corrupting urban economy of exchange and exploitation, and that in reality there was very little that was either natural or moral about rural life: "It was no moral case of God made the country and man made the town" (Williams 1973, 54). The English countryside had been made and remade, and the city was often the agent of rural capitalist development.

By "facts" Williams meant the real events of history; by "perspective" he meant the representation of these events and their circumstances. He read histories as a record and literature as something more than historical evidence. Literary works disclose meanings and signs of a collective memory which require interpretation and analysis.

Williams's reliance on the distinction between literature and historical writing allowed him to produce his critique of ideology. This kind of ideological critique must of necessity be based upon a distinction, problematic though it may be, between "reality" and "distortion." How else could he have known that labor and exploitation were the undertext of the image of the country house?

The aim of Williams's analysis in *The Country and the City* was to view "country" and "city" as two dimensions of a single historical process, and to recover this connection as historical memory. He viewed the history of the relation of country to city as a changing reality and argued that the radical contrast between country and city is one of the major ideological forms in which people have become conscious of their common experience and, presently, of the global crisis of contemporary industrial society. In addition, he intended to put into question commonly held prejudices against rural life within the socialist movement, viewing Marx and Engels's famous remark about the "idiocy of rural life" as emblematic of this prejudice and ultimately divisive to a progressive movement for social change.

The Debate with Marxism

In *The Country and the City* Raymond Williams moved from the analysis of country-house poems to the domain of everyday life. The journey was made difficult by his having begun with the texts of high culture. This problem ironically parallels the analysis in *Culture and Society* in the distinction Williams made in the earlier work between the elitist valuation of culture and culture as a way of life.

Williams argued, in an essay originally published in 1968, that culture is the ordinariness of life among a people, that it expresses a way of life, and that it is not the property of a special elite of writers and critics. The ordinariness of culture does not lie in its received traditions but in its engagement of people and their participation in a shared way of life (Williams 1989b, 32-38). In an essay published in 1983, he criticized Lukacs for not having been able to deal with the cultural dimensions of everyday life and for having remained on the terrain of high culture (Williams 1989c, 274). Williams's own cultural studies, however, suffered from the same failure to bridge the gap between the traditional canon and the way of life. His attempt to articulate a conception of popular culture required a refocus from literary texts to the textuality of everyday life. He recognized this problem but was unable to account sufficiently for the institutional mediations between these two spheres of cultural life. The analysis of literacy and the reading public that appears in *The Long Revolution* provided only the semblance of a bridge rather than a theory of mediation. Such a theory would not simply add a third term; it would have altered the very terms of analysis.

For Williams, *The Country and the City* also marked the beginning of a debate with Marxism. In this work, his engagement with the Marxist tradition took the form of an analysis of the rural-urban nexus in the development of capitalism. In *Culture and Society* he had not treated Marxism as a significant force in British social thought. His discussion of the Marxist literary critics of the 1930s, like Christopher Caudwell, focused upon their superstructural theory of culture without taking their actual studies seriously. By contrast, Williams's theoretical argument in *The Long Revolution* attempted to oppose economic determinism, substituting multiple determinations of culture, politics, economy, and family as an answer to the reductionism of the base-superstructure model of "orthodox Marxism."

Williams's theoretical essays of the 1970s tried to bring his own intellectual project into line with recent developments in Marxist cultural theory. His own earlier cultural studies had lacked a clear theoretical conceptualization. They were detailed, insightful, and nuanced but did not possess a clearly articulated theory of culture consistent with his view of historical change (Williams 1979, 139). His engagement with Marxist cultural theory expressed his opposition to the influence of structuralism upon literary theory in Western Europe and North America (Williams 1979, 339).

In his essay "Base and Superstructure in Marxist Cultural Theory," Williams began by defining the point of entry for a debate within Marxism:

> Any modern approach to a Marxist theory of culture must begin by considering the proposition of a determining base and a determined superstructure. From a strictly theoretical point of view this is not, in fact, where we might choose to begin (Williams 1980, 31).

His suggestion here was that a dialogue with Marxism should begin with the discursive prominence of the relation of base to superstructure. His aim was to put forward a critique of this conception in a way that would allow him to move toward a restatement in terms of the Gramscian notion of hegemony. This very same line of argument was repeated in somewhat greater detail in *Marxism and Literature* (Williams 1977, 75 - 141). There, the critical transformation of the relation of economy to society depended on a noncausal conception of "determination."

Williams redefined "determination" to mean the "setting of limits," thereby departing from the positivist notion of the base as a "fixed economic or technological abstraction." This allowed him to emphasize the human dimension of social practice and therefore the role of agency in history. Culture became understandable as a material process of production rather than a passive result of forces emanating from the economic base (Williams 1980, 34).

Williams articulated what he took to be a culturally relevant and historically adequate conception of hegemony:

> This notion of hegemony as deeply saturating the consciousness of a society seems to me to be fundamental. And hegemony has the advantage over general notions of totality, that it at the same time emphasizes the facts of domination (Williams 1980, 37).

The key terms in this passage are "saturating," "consciousness," and "domination." Williams found Gramsci's conception of hegemony to be one that allowed for a more subtle and dynamic representation of the contradictory meanings, values, and social practices that are the substance of cultural life than the orthodox theory of base causally determining superstructure.

Williams's main contribution to the theory of hegemony was the distinction he made among dominant, residual, and emergent culture. These were understood in terms of an interactive process of struggle. Their interrelations were mediated by existing institutions and social practices and, as a consequence, reflected the operation of human agency as well as relations of power and exploitation. These concepts provided formal analytical tools for Williams's subsequent analysis of culture and politics (Williams 1977, 121-27 and 1980, 37-42).

It may seem ironic that Williams made very little use of the concepts of dominant, residual, and emergent culture in his political analysis of the 1970s and 1980s (Williams 1983b, 1989a). His actual analysis was ad hoc, topical, particular, and reflective; but it was not well grounded in the theory that had been presaged by his critique of economic determinism.

Perhaps his predilection for debate with the main traditions in English social thought rather than with Marxist theory as such was not simply due to a judgment that the former was more politically relevant than the latter. It may be that his reluctance to treat Marxism for its methodological implications reflected his own resistance to theory and preference for the interpretive and the concrete, whether this was "key words" or social and political institutions. His "coming to terms" with cultural theory was only a partial movement from particular analyses to a theoretical framework for the conduct of a more comprehensive intellectual project.

Between Humanism and Theory

In 1961, E. P. Thompson published a two-part review essay of *Culture and Society* and *The Long Revolution* in *New Left Review* (Thompson 1961a, 1961b). Most of his critical remarks focused upon Williams's lack of clarity concerning the class nature of English society. Thompson's focus was upon the conceptions of "the reading public" and "a common culture." He argued that Williams had detached his analysis of the popular press from the history of working-class movements and that he had largely ignored the role of the working-class press of the nineteenth century. Williams's analysis of the popular press, according to Thompson, lacked reference to class struggle. Thompson preferred the definition of culture as "a whole way of struggle" to Williams's "a whole way of life."

Thompson did believe that *Culture and Society* and *The Long Revolution* had made important contributions to the socialist analysis of culture. He saw a close relationship between Williams's and his own understanding of the vital role working-class people play in making their own history; and he agreed with Williams's departure from the simplifications of "orthodox Marxism."

In an essay first published in *New Left Review* in 1975 and later reprinted as part of the first chapter of *Criticism and Ideology* (1978), Terry Eagleton criticized Raymond Williams for reformism and romantic populism, for stressing lived experience over conceptual understanding, for having an organicist conception of culture, and for suffering from an anti-intellectual bias. Eagleton argued that Williams's cultural analysis was ideologically grounded in humanism, idealism, empiricism, and realism. In his view, Williams's literary analysis was too closely linked to the work of F. R. Leavis. *Culture and Society* represented only a partial break with the main traditions in English social thought. In other words, Williams had identified too closely with the very conservative thinkers he had criticized. At this point in his career, Eagleton found little of value in the cultural criticism of his former teacher and colleague at Cambridge.

In an essay entitled "Romanticism, Moralism and Utopianism: The Case of William Morris" (Thompson 1976), Thompson defended Williams against what he saw as Eagleton's sectarian criticism by arguing that Eagleton's position was that of an "elitism of theory." This polemic was part of his general criticism of Althusserian Marxism (Thompson 1978). Thompson's primary aim was to defend Marxian humanism against structuralist Marxism and he saw Williams as a comrade in this struggle.

In the same issue of *New Left Review*, Anthony Barnett argued in contrast to Thompson that Eagleton had reduced the concept of culture to the Althusserian notion of ideology (Barnett 1976). Barnett argued that the main weakness of Williams's analysis of culture was his failure to theorize the relationship between culture and politics. It was not that Williams had denied the political dimension of cultural life. He agreed with Eagleton that Williams's analysis suffered from "culturalism," the tendency to explain historical change by identifying culture as the moving force of history. Culturalism was simply the inverse of economism. One was no more dynamic than the other as a theory of historical change.

In a more temperate essay written after Raymond Williams's death (Eagleton 1988), Eagleton rethought his critique in the light of a greater appreciation of Williams's personal and moral commitment to the socialist project, and took up Williams's own project of combining a close reading of texts with a social analysis of contexts and institutions. Eagleton modified the tone of his earlier criticism and largely abandoned the paradigm of Althusserian Marxism. This essay reflected a change in Eagleton's political and philosophical stance as much as it did a changed evaluation of the work of Raymond Williams.

The critical discussion of the work of Raymond Williams points to a very real problem: the relationship between humanism and theory. The debate over the merits of Williams's analysis of culture has not answered the theoretical or practical problems articulated by the terms of this discussion. His analysis of culture took place within the tension between moral commitment and theory.

Most of Williams's cultural analysis was firmly on the side of humanism and in opposition to what he took to be the abstractions of theory. He was reluctant to speculate in philosophical terms about the nature of language, society, or historical change. His theoretical writings of the 1970s (Williams 1977, 1980) were an attempt to come to terms with both Marxism and his own earlier work. In my view, these theoretical reflections stopped short of completing this project. They also remain isolated from his political and cultural analyses.

Unlike Thompson, Raymond Williams opposed Althusserian structuralism without the excesses of polemic that characterized Thompson's writings of the late 1970s. This is clear when we compare *Marxism and Literature* (Williams 1977) with *The Poverty of Theory* (Thompson 1978). In *Marxism and Literature*, Williams opposed structuralism by rethinking the base and superstructure model and by formulating an alternative conception of cultural domination. Thompson's response to structuralism was defensive, overly subjective, and took the form of an altogether immoderate polemic. He offered a defense of humanism against what he took to be the "elitism of theory." While Williams moved toward a theoretical conception of culture and a reworking of the problem of hegemony, Thompson seemed to reject the importance of theoretical concerns for the analysis of culture and politics. It is, however, Williams's influence that remains powerful in contemporary cultural studies, with their emphasis on the counterhegemonies of feminist, Third World, and working-class movements.

REFERENCES

Barnett, A. 1976. "Raymond Williams and Marxism: A Rejoinder to Terry
    Eagleton." *New Left Review,* no. 99. (September-October): 47-64.
Eagleton, T. 1978. *Criticism and Ideology.* London: Verso.
_____. 1988. "Resources for a Journey of Hope: The Significance of Raymond
    Williams." *New Left Review,* no. 168 (March-April): 3-11.
Thompson, E.P. 1961a. "The Long Revolution I." *New Left Review,* no. 9
    (September-October): 24-33.
_____. 1961b. "The Long Revolution II." *New Left Review,* no. 10 (November-
    December): 34-39.
_____. 1976. "Romanticism, Moralism and Utopianism: The Case of William
    Morris." *New Left Review,* no. 99. (September-October): 83-114.
_____. 1978. *The Poverty of Theory.* New York: Monthly Review Press.
Williams, R. 1961. *The Long Revolution.* New York: Columbia University
    Press.
_____. 1966. *Modern Tragedy.* Stanford: Stanford University Press.
_____. 1970. *The English Novel from Dickens to Lawrence.* London: Chatto &
    Windus.
_____. 1973. *The Country and the City.* New York: Oxford University Press.
_____. 1976. *Keywords.* New York: Oxford University Press.
_____. 1977. *Marxism and Literature.* New York: Oxford University Press.
_____. 1979. *Politics and Letters.* London: Verso.

_____. 1980. *Problems in Materialism and Culture.* London: Verso.
_____. 1983a. *Culture and Society.* New York: Columbia University Press.
_____. 1983b. *The Year 2000.* New York: Pantheon.
_____. 1989a. *The Politics of Modernism.* London: Verso.
_____. 1989b. *Resources of Hope.* London: Verso.
_____. 1989c. *What I Came to Say.* London: Hutchinson Radius.

CHAPTER 5

Defending the Enlightenment:
Jürgen Habermas and the
Theory of Communicative Reason

Introduction

Jürgen Habermas's writings on postmodernism lack the subtle reasoning of his other works in philosophy and social theory. His analyses of Derrida and Foucault are attempts to warn the reader against the political dangers of philosophical irrationalism. What is at stake for Habermas is more than a critical exchange. It is in this sense that his *The Philosophical Discourse of Modernity* can be compared with Georg Lukacs's *The Destruction of Reason*. Neither work is simply a narrative history of Western philosophy.

Unlike Lukacs, Habermas has little to say about the role played by literature or the arts. Modernity is for Habermas both a historical period and a philosophical discourse which he traces to Kant and Hegel and the split between the Left and Right Hegelians. As in the case of Lukacs, Nietzsche is a pivotal figure in the development of anti-Hegelian critiques of reason. For Lukacs, the political dangers were clear to all: Fascism and the cold war.

For readers of Habermas, the central problem represented by postmodernism is not immediately evident. He views postmodern social critics as neoconservatives. However, this does not mean that they are consciously aware of playing this role. Most postmodernists see themselves as rebels against the established order of bourgeois society. They are at war (at least in theory) with Western culture from antiquity to the 20th century. They are critics of the Enlightenment, progress, and the very concept of reason. This is precisely where Lyotard, Derrida, and Foucault part company with Habermas.

Habermas defends the Enlightenment and the concept of reason against its new critics. What he fears is the return to the kind of barbarism which was embodied in the Nazi movement. This is clear from his debate with revisionist German historians like Ernst Nolte and Michael Sturmer (Habermas 1990, chapter 9). For Habermas, there is something more at stake in postmodernism than academic philosophy or cultural criticism. Hence his stand on the side of liberal democracy.

The theoretical question raised by Habermas's own position is the power of ideas to transform history for good or evil. Unlike Lukacs, Habermas provides no analysis of class struggle or the crisis of capitalism. His own analysis has displaced capitalism to the margins of intellectual discourse. The central problematic of his social theory is modernity and the achievement of moral consensus through argument and discussion.

My primary aim in this essay is to provide an overview of Habermas's social theory and his defense of the Enlightenment against postmodernism. In my own view, neither Habermas nor the postmodernists have provided an adequate conception of late capitalism and the political and moral dilemmas faced by the Left during a period of global capital hegemony.

The Rise and Fall of the Public Space

The Structural Transformation of the Public Sphere was originally published in 1962. An English translation did not become available until 1989. This book is significant because it expresses many of the author's political concerns about power, communication and the role of civil society. *The Structural Transformation of the Public Sphere* articulates an analysis of the problem of communication within modern society. However, in 1962, Habermas had not yet developed a theory of "communicative reason" or "discourse ethics."

He presents an account of the emergence, transformation and disintegration of the bourgeois public sphere in England, France and Germany in the 18th and 19th centuries, arguing that the liberal public sphere occupied the discursive space between the state and civil society. Within this space, critical public discussion of matters of political interest was institutionally guaranteed. The liberal public sphere was formed in the historic circumstances of a developing market economy. State authority was publicly monitored through this dissemination of information and critical reflection. Habermas traces the interdependent development of the literary and political self-consciousness of the bourgeoisie, while noting the contradiction between the rights granted and their restriction to a specific social class.

According to Habermas, the intermingling of state and civil society in the late 19th and early 20th centuries led to the demise of the liberal public sphere which had depended upon the separation of state and society. The result, institutionally, was the social democratic welfare state. This new political situation is defined by competition among conflicting interest groups which negotiate and make compromises with government officials while excluding the public from this process:

> Citizens entitled to services relate to the state not primarily through political participation but by adopting a general attitude of demand— expecting to be provided for, without actually wanting to fight for the necessary decisions. Their contact with the state occurs essentially in the rooms and anterooms of bureaucracies; it is unpolitical and indifferent, yet demanding (Habermas 1989, 211).

In the new situation, the press and broadcast media serve less as organizations of public information and debate than as techniques for managing consensus and promoting a consumer culture. The active participation of citizens within the public sphere has been replaced by manipulation. As Habermas puts it:

> Because private enterprises evoke in their customers the idea that in their consumption decisions they act in their capacity as citizens, the state has to "address" its citizens like consumers (Habermas 1989, 211).

In a post-liberal era, the question emerges whether the classical model of the public sphere is any longer feasible as a political ideal. The issue Habermas raises is whether or not a public sphere can be constituted under radically different socio-economic, political and cultural conditions. This is a question he raises but does not answer within the framework of the historical narrative which he has used to ground his account.

In the essays contained in *Toward a Rational Society*, Habermas articulates a conception of both technical domination and a theory of communicative action. The themes of purposive rationality and discursive will formation have occupied him for the last thirty-five years. His entire work can be understood in terms of a transcendental logic of reason, morality and politics. In the 1970s and '80s, he carried on a debate with both neoconservatives in Germany and the United States and French postmodernist cultural critics. It is in the context of this debate that he has attempted to formulate a defense of the Enlightenment in terms of a theory of communicative reason.

Habermas has accepted the postmodernist critique of the essentialism implicit in the philosophy of consciousness. However, this has not led him to embrace a philosophy of language freed from the constraints of labor and power. These themes have remained central to his work from *Knowledge and Human Interest* and *On the Logic of the Social Sciences* through the two volumes of *The Theory of Communicative Action* to *The Philosophical Discourse of Modernity* and *The New Conservatism*. His alternative to the philosophy of consciousness is a conception of communicative action which is structured both by the lifeworld and the constraints of the social system.

Lukacs and Habermas on Irrationalism

In *Critical Theory, Marxism and Modernity* (Kellner 1989), Douglas Kellner has criticized Habermas for failing to appreciate the cultural fabric of late capitalism. He situates Habermas's critique of postmodernism within the tradition of Critical Theory and, in particular, Adorno's and Horkheimer's analysis of reification, the consumer society and the administered life. Like many other commentators, Kellner does not see the more obvious connection between Habermas and Lukacs.

In a polemical review of *The Meaning of Contemporary Realism* (Adorno 1977), Adorno suggested that Lukacs had abandoned his own reason in the analysis of modern philosophy contained in *The Destruction of Reason*. After praising the cultural criticism of the young Lukacs, Adorno proceeded to attack him for what he took to be the dogmatic rejection of 19th- and 20th-century philosophy and modernist literature. Against the view of Lukacs, Adorno continued to assert that the autonomy of modern art was the one remaining critical moment within bourgeois culture. Lukacs had rejected both the conception of the autonomy of artistic production and the idea that there was anything critical in the perspective of writers like James Joyce and Samuel Beckett. Lukacs's defense of Critical Realism against both Naturalism and Modernism depended on an appeal to a subject/object dialectic embodied in literary narrative.

One of the reasons that Habermas's defense of modernity is often linked with Adorno's aesthetic modernism has to do with the choice of terms for his analysis. Lukacs's defense of the Enlightenment followed the line of his aesthetic and epistemological conception of realism. The critique of irrationalism, expressed in *The Destruction of Reason* and in his literary studies from the 1930s through the 1950s, can be understood as a defense of the possibility of knowledge and human progress.

Habermas's own defense of the Enlightenment takes the form of a conception of modernity which he adopts from Kant and Weber. This conception equates modern society with the autonomous spheres of science, morality and art. His critique of postmodernism actually has little in common with the aesthetic debate between Lukacs and Adorno over the value of modern art. Instead, it has a great deal to do with conceptions of reason and progress.

Many who continue to write within the tradition of Critical Theory have accepted both Adorno's philosophy of aesthetics and his attitude toward Lukacs's alleged "Stalinism." When Adorno read *The Destruction of Reason,* he failed to place it within its proper historical context: the rise of Fascism and the early years of the cold war. His criticism of Lukacs involved a reading which abstracted statements, arguments and conclusions from the immediacy of a complex and desperate political struggle. He read *The Destruction of Reason* as if it were just another poorly written history of European philosophy rather than as an intervention with a specific project. This may have influenced Habermas's own failure to see the connection between his and Lukacs's analysis of irrationalism.

In *The Destruction of Reason,* Lukacs traced the development of bourgeois thought in three fields: philosophy, sociology and racial theory. If we include his literary studies, the story is told yet a fourth time. This narrative is what self-conscious postmodernists, like Lyotard, would call a metanarrative, as if it had no aim but that of regulating all discourses. Lukacs's analysis of irrationalism was written in the name of progress and a common humanity.

The figure of Nietzsche plays a central role for both Lukacs and Habermas. For Lukacs, the turning point for the European bourgeoisie was the challenge of the revolutions of 1848, after which irrationalism came to dominate bourgeois discourse. Lukacs claimed that Nietzsche was the dominant figure of irrationalist philosophy during the imperialist period from 1870 through World War I, not merely for what he wrote but for the way he was read and interpreted. He represented the alternative in philosophical terms to socialism, democracy and fundamental human equality.

Habermas's own historiography outlines two paths, both of which draw upon Nietzsche's philosophy. The first goes from Heidegger to Derrida, and the second from Bataille to Foucault. Habermas's narrative simultaneously constitutes a history of ideas and a critique of ideology. He traces the decline of reason from Nietzsche to postmodernism in terms of "modernism" and "postmodernism" which represent the dangers of irrational discourse and a politics of nihilism.

Lukacs's text provides more than a history of ideas; it places these ideas within a historical context. He discusses the decay of bourgeois intellectual and moral standards in terms of both epistemology and aesthetics and emphasizes the relationship between intellectual production and the reality of class struggle. In contrast, class struggle does not play an important role in Habermas's analysis of postmodernism. Instead of emphasizing the political and economic crisis which characterizes late capitalism, he emphasizes moral commitment to reason or the loss of faith in the project of Enlightenment.

Habermas goes as far as suggesting that postmodernism is simply another form of neoconservative ideology. In *The Philosophical Discourse of Modernity*, he remarks:

> We cannot exclude from the outset the possibility that neoconservatism and aesthetically inspired anarchism, in the name of a farewell to modernity, are merely trying to revolt against it once again. It could be that they are merely cloaking their complicity with the venerable tradition of counter-Enlightenment in the garb of post-Enlightenment (Habermas 1987, 5).

In this passage Habermas equates Arnold Gehlen and Daniel Bell with Jacques Derrida and Michel Foucault. Jean-Francois Lyotard has criticized Habermas for suggesting that postmodernists are only neoconservatives in disguise (Lyotard 1984, 73).

What is Modernity?

In the *Philosophical Discourse of Modernity*, Habermas devotes a chapter to the discussion of *The Dialectic of Enlightenment.* The importance of this chapter is that it clearly separates his own understanding of the Enlightenment from that of Horkheimer and Adorno. He argues that theirs is a one-sided view of modernity that over-emphasizes the role of instrumental reason and the domination over nature. He does not deny this feature of the Enlightenment but argues that it does not exhaust the concept of modernity.

Habermas argues that in *The Dialectic of Enlightenment*, Horkheimer and Adorno characterized the Enlightenment's process of self-development in such a way that their analysis made it no longer possible to place any hope in the liberating force of modernity. What was left unexamined was their elision of the achievements of Occidental Rationalism. Horkheimer and Adorno failed to appreciate the rational content of cultural modernity. All they could see was the relationship of purposive rationalism to domination:

> The critical capacity to take up a "Yes" or "No" stance and to distinguish between valid and invalid propositions is undermined as power and validity claims enter into a turbid fashion (Habermas 1987, 112).

In Habermas's view, *The Dialectic of Enlightenment* did not do justice to the rational content of modernity that was expressed in bourgeois ideals.

Habermas argues that the methods of analysis and presentation in *The Dialectic of Enlightenment* are similar to those of Nietzsche. As he puts it:

> Point-for-point correspondence with Nietzsche are found in the construction by which Horkheimer and Adorno underpin their "primal history of subjectivity" (Habermas 1987, 121).

Moreover, Habermas believes that Horkheimer's and Adorno's methods reduce philosophical argument to a literary criticism in which historical analysis gets lost in a poetics of history. Reason is divorced from its central role in the philosophical discourse of modernity whose origin Habermas locates in Kant's 1784 essay, "What is Enlightenment?" (Kant 1963, 3-10).

Habermas's own conception of modernity is drawn from his reading of European philosophy and sociology, from Kant and Hegel to Max Weber. Weber, rather than Marx, plays a central role, along with Kant, in Habermas's conception of modernity:

> What Weber depicted was not only the secularization of Western culture but also and especially the development of modern societies from the viewpoint of rationalization (Habermas 1987, 1).

Habermas argues that modern empirical science, autonomous art and theories of morality and law can be understood as three separate cultural spheres historically grounded in the evolution of society. Each grounded the learning processes that increased the complexity and coordination of modern social organization. Thus, Habermas's view of modernity locates Weber's conception of autonomous cultural spheres within the framework of a theory of social evolution.

In 1980 Habermas was awarded the Adorno prize. In his acceptance speech, he asserted his own commitment to the project of modernity and argued that rather than giving up on the Enlightenment as a lost cause, we should learn from its excesses. In his view, the philosophers of the Enlightenment wanted to utilize their intellectual powers for the enrichment of everyday life and the rational organization of society.

The Enlightenment project of modernity was to develop an objective science, a universal morality, and an autonomous sphere of art. In Habermas's view, Weber's characterization of cultural modernity as the separation of substantive reason expressed in religion and metaphysics into the three autonomous spheres of science, morality and art was consistent with this project. The unified conception of ontology and epistemology collapsed (Habermas 1981, 8) as religion and metaphysics became the central targets of philosophical criticism during the 18th century.

It was in this context that Kant attempted to provide a transcendental justification for science, morality and art in *The Critique of Pure Reason*, *The Critique of Practical Reason* and *The Critique of Judgment*. This was also the context of Kant's political writings, of which his essay "What is Enlightenment?" is particularly important. When Habermas speaks of the Enlightenment, he is usually referring to the German rather than the French or English Enlightenment—to Kant rather than Rousseau, Diderot or Francis Bacon.

Kant's central argument in "What is Enlightenment?" has to do with the significance of intellectual freedom. He opposed any form of government censorship which would interfere with the freedom of intellectuals to debate the important issues of the day. He also argued that the unenlightened citizen would be dependent upon others to define moral standards and ultimate truth and therefore could not be a moral agent. What Kant was essentially defending was the freedom of intellectuals and the possibility of an argument rather than the authority of tradition. This conception of rational discourse forms the basis for Habermas's own identification and analysis of communicative reason. His advance beyond Kant's original formulation consists in going beyond the abstract and idealized conception of rational consciousness in favor of an alternative conception of intersubjective rational dialogue.

Communicative Reason and Discourse Ethics

Rejecting postmodernism's critique of rationality, Habermas argues for a conception of politics and society that reflects both the Enlightenment's emphasis on reason and the post-modernist critique of the failure of rationalists to take account of power and ideology. Although Habermas has moved closer to Kant's conception of epistemology and ethics, his aim has been to reformulate the idea of reason in terms of a theory of communicative reason and discourse ethics. Kant's conception of abstract reason has been replaced by intersubjectivity and rational consensus.

At various times, Habermas has referred to his own contribution to Critical Theory as "the theory of undistorted communication," "communicative reason" and "discourse ethics." All of these derive loosely from his notion of an "ideal speech situation" implicit in all instances of communication and free in principle from political coercion and distortion. His primary model for the analysis of communicative reason is the therapeutic relationship between doctor and patient. Psychoanalysis provides the referent of a conceptual model for achieving undistorted communication. This can be distinguished from the clinical practice of psychoanalytic treatment where the doctor-patient relationship is one of an inequality of knowledge and insight. Moreover, since the patient enters this relationship in order to obtain relief from emotional distress, it lacks the initial conditions of uncoerced consensus among participants.

Fundamental to Habermas's analysis of communicative reason is the assumption that mutual understanding is possible under the conditions of rational argument provided by genuine dialogue. The very practice of such dialogue is the ongoing accomplishment of consensus and the rejection of coercion and manipulation. In this "ideal speech situation," normative claims to validity must be based upon the quality of an argument. As Habermas puts it in *Moral Consciousness and Communicative Action:* "Ultimately, there is only one criterion by which beliefs can be judged valid, and that is that they are based on agreement reached by argumentation" (Habermas 1990, 14). That is, consensus for Habermas is always predicated on a prior consensus, dialogue on a prior dialogue.

For Habermas, everyday communication makes possible the kind of understanding that is, in principle, based upon claims of validity. It provides the only real alternative to exercising influence in a more coercive way. It is important to understand that, for Habermas, "communicative reason" refers to the conditions necessary for understanding to be arrived at discursively, through dialogue. He says, in *The Philosophical Discourse of Modernity:* "Reason is by its very nature incarnated in contexts of communicative action and in structures of the lifeworld" (Habermas 1987, 322). This expresses his aim to establish the premises of his conception of "discourse ethics."

Habermas links his conception of "communicative reason" with "discourse ethics" by arguing that the former is possible only if all participants take part in a cooperative search for truth. As he puts it:

> The thesis that discourse ethics puts forth is that anyone who seriously undertakes to participate in argumentation implicitly accepts by that very undertaking general pragmatic presuppositions that have a normative content (Habermas 1990, 197-198).

For Habermas, the concept of discourse ethics represents an attempt to rethink the Enlightenment project of reason and morality in terms of a sociology of discourse. Thus, it involves an articulation of intersubjectivity and dialogue, and a demonstration as the basis for progress, democracy and reason.

For Habermas, discourse ethics replaces the Kantian categorical imperative with a noncategorical process, that of moral argumentation, and the value of consequences, with the value of dialogue. He asserts that the very participation in dialogue entails accepting a norm of participation. This normative content is defined by validity claims that each speaker must be taken to have accepted as both rational to and necessary for the attainment of consensus without recourse to coercion or manipulation. The validity claims which form the explicit normative structure of argumentation are not, themselves, justified by reference to a process of dialogue, but are, rather, derived philosophically as the necessary prior condition for achieving consensus. It does not follow, however, that they are not the historical *result* of dialogue. In this, Habermas respects the distinction between history and the use of reason necessary to protect reason as a value in its own right. In this way, Habermas comes full circle: reason is a product of history, but it has its own imperatives and a justification that is beyond history. For him, reason has become the absolute value through which human consciousness derives the possibility of self-reflection and progress.

Like Kant, Habermas has provided a series of universal ethical principles. Unlike Kant, these are historical as well as absolute. For Kant, ethical principles are exercised by the individual will in the practical activity of daily life. For Habermas, rational validity claims establish the moral ground for the practical activity of communication and action within the lifeworld. One question raised by this move is whether Habermas has succeeded in transforming Kant's idealized abstract individual into something living, or has merely shifted the ground to equally idealized abstractions of intersubjectivity and dialogue.

Habermas accepts many of the arguments of Richard Rorty in *Philosophy and the Mirror of Nature*, particularly that the role Kant had attributed to philosophy was altogether too grand. However, he stops short of accepting Rorty's view that philosophy can make no claim to establishing truth. In Habermas's view, philosophy remains the guardian of reason. As he puts it: "...the basic phenomenon that moral philosophy must explain is the normative validity (*Sollgetung*) of commands and norms of action" (Habermas 1990, 196).

Habermas's theory of communication is normative, not descriptive. His conception of the "ideal speech situation" allows him to evaluate actual processes of intersubjective communication as departures from rationality. It also allows him to evaluate the ethical dimensions of everyday life in modern society from the perspective of a model of rational argumentation consistent with fundamental democratic principles.

It is not clear what kind of collective practice would logically follow from the moral judgments Habermas has made about the process of achieving an uncoerced consensus. The problem is what position Critical Theory will take when social movements do not live up to the standards established by a theory of communicative reason that transcends the practices of everyday life, and formulates the ideas of communication as an abstraction against its own history, free from the distorting effects of actual power relations.

Postmodernism and the Critique of Metanarratives

The Postmodern Condition by Jean-Francois Lyotard is a report on the prospects for science and education in postindustrial society. Lyotard argues that both functionalism and neo-Marxist social theory articulate a conception of society as an organic totality and that both theories have been incorporated into the administrative control over daily life. He concludes that both welfare-state liberalism and socialism have been made obsolete by the postmodern conditions of knowledge and communication.

Against Habermas's theory of communicative reason and discourse ethics, Lyotard argues that a series of language games defines social bonds in postmodern society. In his view, legitimation results from the linguistic practices of communication within daily life. The social division of labor of a postmodern society requires narratives that can both provide a means of communication and a sense of personal identity and social location.

Against Habermas's version of critical theory, Lyotard asserts:

> We no longer have recourse to the grand narratives—we can resort
> neither to the dialectic of Spirit nor even to the emancipation of humanity
> (Lyotard 1984, 60).

He goes on to argue:

> It seems neither possible, nor even prudent, to follow Habermas in
> orienting our treatment of the problem of legitimation in the direction
> of a search for universal consensus through what he calls *Diskurs*, in
> other words, a dialogue of argumentation (Lyotard 1984, 65).

Lyotard offers a conception of restricted language games as an alternative
to Habermas's transcendental conception of the necessary conditions for
achieving undistorted communication. He rejects Habermas's theory of
consensus as hopelessly embedded in the metaphysics of the subject and
a teleological theory of history.

In his defense of the postmodern conception of liberty, Lyotard
exaggerates the organic underpinning of Habermas's theory of modernity.
He argues that there is a greater unity between science, ethics and art than
Habermas actually suggests. He goes as far as asserting:

> What Habermas requires from the arts and the experiences they provide
> is, in short, to bridge the gap between cognitive, ethical, and political
> discourses. Thus opening the way to a unity of experience (Lyotard
> 1984, 72).

Habermas does not articulate a conception of aesthetics which could
possibly perform the task of unification. Instead, he offers a theory of
dialogue which is grounded in a transcendental conception of validity.
For Habermas, the fundamental problem is not in proposing a means of
unifying experience, but rather in conceptualizing the necessary conditions
which would make a democratically achieved consensus possible.

The heart of Lyotard's polemic against Habermas lies in the political
and philosophical rejection of the concept of totality. He argues that the
metanarrative of human emancipation can only result in political
oppression and tyranny over the individual. As he puts it:

> The nineteenth and twentieth centuries have given us as much terror as
> we can take. We have paid a high enough price for the nostalgia of the
> whole and the one (Lyotard 1984, 81).

Like Horkheimer and Adorno, Lyotard asserts a rather simplistic causal theory of political oppression. This theory suggests that the horrors of violence and political repression which have defined much of the 20th century are the consequences of the Enlightenment project of reason and domination over nature. For Lyotard, there is a political alternative to the tyranny of the concept:

> The answer is: Let us wage war on totality; let us be witnesses to the unpresentable; let us activate the differences and save the honor of the name (Lyotard 1984, 82).

The irony in Lyotard's analysis of postindustrial society is that it is premised upon a faith in science and education. There was nothing more sacred to the Enlightenment project of human emancipation through reason than the freedom which would result from the unfettered development of science and education. It would seem that Lyotard remains trapped within the very discourse of progress he has attempted to deconstruct in the name of a postmodern conception of liberty. It is also not clear how the postmodern conception of liberty can be philosophically grounded outside an historical project of emancipation. It can, of course, be expressed untheoretically in the language game known as "common sense."

Richard Rorty agrees with the main tenets of Lyotard's critique of Habermas's theory of communication. However, he avoids Lyotard's conclusion that totalitarianism results from metanarratives of human emancipation. Instead, Rorty argues that philosophy may have little relation to politics. As he puts it:

> What links Habermas to the French thinkers he criticizes is the conviction that the story of modern philosophy (as successive reactions to Kant's diremptions) is an important part of the story of the democratic societies' attempts at self-reassurance. But it may be that most of the latter story could be told as the history of reformist politics, without much reference to the kinds of theoretical backup which philosophers have provided for such politics (Bernstein 1985, 169).

Rorty argues that for Habermas, abandoning a standpoint which is universalistic betrays the social hopes which have been central to liberal politics. He goes on to argue that liberal-democratic politics may not be dependent upon philosophical grounds. In other words, Habermas's concern with elaborating a philosophical defense of the Enlightenment project of human emancipation may simply be irrelevant to the political project of democracy. Instead of metanarratives being the source of 20th century tyranny, they are simply an irrelevant reflection upon the premises which would constitute the grounds for a liberal democratic social order under the conditions of postmodernism. After having rejected the importance of philosophical discourse to the political life of a society, it is not clear what role philosophy could claim for itself. Like Lyotard, Rorty ends up with a common-sense faith in liberty and the prospects for democratic society.

Both Richard Bernstein and Albrecht Wellmer have attempted to defend Habermas against his postmodern critics. Bernstein has argued that making judgments about the pathological features of modernity presupposes a normative standard for judging what is pathological or deformed. He believes that Habermas's theory of communicative action provides such a standard. This standard for judgment is the validity claims of comprehensibility, truth, sincerity and appropriateness (Bernstein 1985, 18).

Bernstein argues that Habermas's theory of communicative action is a "reconstructive science" which seeks to isolate, identify and clarify the conditions required for undistorted communication. He argues that emancipatory self-reflection is dependent upon giving a rational reconstruction of the universal conditions for communicative reason. As he puts it:

> For it is only in and through dialogue that one can achieve self-understanding. If dialogue is not to be an empty impotent deal, then a transformation and reconstruction of the social institutions and practices in which dialogic communication is embedded becomes a practical imperative (Bernstein 1985, 12).

The problem with this kind of formulation is that it remains on the level of philosophical abstraction and does not deal with the problems of historical agency other than by asserting the necessity for rational communication. It offers a standard of judgment for the social critic.

Wellmer has argued that Habermas has translated the project of a Critical Theory of society from a philosophy of consciousness into a theory of language and communication He goes on to argue that Habermas's notion of communicative reason is implicitly grounded in the structure of human speech. Here, Wellmer is asserting the philosophical anthropology which underlies Habermas's theory of language. However, the main aim of Wellmer's discussion is to argue that no claim to validity can be exempt from critical examination by participants. He argues that in Habermas's reconstruction of Critical Theory, Marx's idea of a free association of producers is reinterpreted as the condition of undistorted communication. As Wellmer puts it:

> In an emancipated society the life-world would no longer be subjected to the imperatives of system maintenance; a rationalized life-world would rather subject the systemic mechanism to the needs of the associated individuals (Bernstein 1985, 57).

Using the conceptual framework of Habermas's theory of communicative action, Wellmer equates socialism with a lifeworld free from the coercion of the steering mechanisms of "money and power." This formulation clearly embodies the utopian hopes of Critical Theory.

I doubt that either Lyotard or Rorty would be much impressed by Bernstein's or Wellmer's defense of Habermas, since this defense only restates the premises of Habermas's argument. Bernstein and Wellmer have defended the role Habermas has assigned to philosophy, as the guardian of reason. For postmodernists like Lyotard and Rorty, this is the central problem; arguments grounded in reason cannot provide a credible defense of metanarratives.

REFERENCES

Adorno, Theodor W. 1977. "Reconciliation under Duress," *Aesthetics and Politics*, Ernst Bloch et al. New York: Verso.

Bernstein, Richard J. (ed). 1985. *Habermas and Modernity*. Cambridge: MIT Press.

Habermas, Jürgen. 1970a. *Towards a Rational Society*. Boston: Beacon Press.

_____. 1970b. "Toward a Theory of Communicative Competence," *Recent Sociology*, No. 2: *Patterns of Communicative Behavior*, Hans Peter Dreitzel (ed.). New York: Macmillan.

_____. 1971. *Knowledge and Human Interest*. Boston: Beacon Press.

_____. 1973. *Theory and Practice*. Boston: Beacon Press.

_____. 1975. *Legitimation Crisis*. Boston: Beacon Press.

_____. 1979. *Communication and the Evolution of Society*. Boston: Beacon Press.

_____. 1981. "Modernity versus Postmodernity," *New German Critique*, No. 22. New York.

____. 1985a. *The Theory of Communicative Action*, vol. I: *The Rationalization of Society.* Boston: Beacon Press.

____. 1987. *The Philosophical Discourse of Modernity.* Cambridge: MIT Press.

____. 1988. *On the Logic of the Social Sciences.* Cambridge: MIT Press.

____. 1989a. *The Theory of Communicative Action,* vol. II: *Lifeworld and System: A Critique of Functionalist Reason.* Boston: Beacon Press.

____. 1989b. *The Structural Transformation of the Public Sphere.* Cambridge: MIT Press.

____. 1989c. *The New Conservatism.* Cambridge: MIT Press.

____. 1990. *Moral Consciousness and the Theory of Communicative Action.* Cambridge: MIT Press.

Horkheimer, Max and Theodor W. Adorno. 1975. *Dialectic of Enlightenment.* New York: Continuum.

Kant, Immanuel. 1963. *Kant on History.* New York; Macmillan.

Kellner, Douglas. 1989. *Critical Theory, Marxism, and Modernity.* Baltimore: John Hopkins.

Lukacs, Georg. 1963. *The Meaning of Contemporary Realism.* London: Merlin press.

____. 1981. *The Destruction of Reason.* Atlantic Highlands: Humanities Press.

Lyotard, Jean-Francois. 1984. *The Postmodern Condition: A Report on Knowledge.* Minneapolis: University of Minnesota Press.

Rorty, Richard. 1981. *Philosophy and the Mirror of Nature.* Princeton: Princeton University Press.

CHAPTER 6

Capitalism, Racism and the Struggle for Democracy

Critique of the Caste Model of Race Relations

Oliver Cox began writing about race relations in the early 1940s. Since there was no theoretically satisfactory formulation available at that time, many sociologists adopted the caste model to fill the void. This account originated in the late 1930s and early 1940s, and is represented in the work of W. Lloyd Warner, Robert E. Park, and Gunnar Myrdal, among others. Myrdal's classic, *An American Dilemma*, was by far the most influential study of race relations of the period, and it was the subject of one of Cox's most important critical essays.

The caste model relied on an analogy between race relations in the southern United States and the caste system of India in order to draw attention to one important aspect of race relations: the fact that discrimination by race had been institutionalized as an absolute difference between groups based on ascribed rather than achieved attributes. Although this theory had a general appeal among liberal social scientists, its use of the analogy begged key questions about the nature and dynamics of race relations as such. It identified the essence of racism by a description of its most visible manifestation, its intractability in the context of American society.

During the early 1940s, Cox wrote several essays, most of which were included as chapters in *Caste, Class and Race*, on the use of the analogy to account for race relations. His major argument was that it was inappropriate to apply the concept of caste to a society defined by capitalist class relations:

> The caste system is not merely an attribute of society; it is itself a type of society. It will make no sense at all to speak of a caste society as an

attribute of a capitalist society. These two are distinct social systems, with entirely independent cultural histories and with mutually antagonistic social norms. It is beyond all social logic, moreover, to conceive of a caste system developing spontaneously within a capitalist system (Cox 1970, 541-2).

This amounted to claiming that the analogy confused rather than clarified the issue of race relations and mystified what, in a capitalist society, was distinctly relevant to an adequate account.

The question was not simply whether or not race relations in the United States were rigid and intractable but how these aspects were to be understood. Cox's essay on Myrdal's *An American Dilemma* was first published in 1944. It was his most important attack upon the caste analogy and made three basic claims: (1) that Myrdal ignored the class nature of race relations; (2) that the use of the caste model mystified the real determinants of these relations; and (3) that Myrdal was mistaken in concluding that poor whites were the primary actors in the racial oppression of black Americans while upper-class whites only benefited psychologically, not economically, from the existence of racism.

Cox directed his most trenchant criticism at Myrdal's theoretical framework, particularly the key concepts of the American creed and caste. Myrdal assumed rather than demonstrated the existence of a common American ideology that he called "the American creed" and which he characterized as a fundamental commitment to the civic values of democracy and social equality. It is in regard to this putative commitment that Myrdal was able to depict racial discrimination as a moral dilemma:

> In his attempt to explain race relations in the United States the author seems to have been confronted with two principal problems: (a) the problem of avoiding a political-class interpretation, and (b) the problem of finding an acceptable moral or ethical interpretation (Cox 1970, 509).

Cox contended that Myrdal's use of the analogy of caste was intended to account for racism as an exception to fundamental American values rather than something intrinsic to the social system itself. He concluded that:

> One primary objection to the use of the caste belief in the study of race relations rests not so much upon its scientific untenability as upon its insidious potentialities. It lumps all white people and all Negroes into two antagonistic groups struggling in the interest of a mysterious god

called caste. This is very much to the liking of the exploiters of labor, since it tends to confuse them in an emotional matrix with all the people. ... It thus appears that if white people were not so wicked, if they would only cease wanting to "exalt" themselves and accept the "American Creed," race prejudice would vanish from America (Cox 1970, 520).

Underlying the apparent optimism of those who accounted for race relations in terms of caste, there remained a basic pessimism concerning the possibilities for social change. Racism was understood either as a universal feature of human society or as an irrational aspect of social life. In either case the elimination of prejudice was a utopian rather than an authentically practical socio-political project. This critique reflected Cox's own theoretical position, that the origins and function of racism were to be found in the nature of capitalism and that the abolition of racism depended upon the dynamics of the class struggle.

Cox's analysis of Myrdal's argument had much in common with Marx's critique of classical economics in that the aim of both was to work through the ideological content of what purported to be a theory and to identify the real social relations that underlay both the phenomenon and the theory. This allowed for a formulation of concepts adequate to the object of investigation.

Capitalism and Racism

Cox began his analysis of the relationship between capitalism and racism by denying that there was anything universal or natural about prejudice against a people because of skin color. He argued that modern racism is an ideology that developed in Europe only with the rise of capitalism and nationalism. According to Cox, racial antagonism as such did not exist before the fifteenth century. Earlier societies in Greece, Rome, and during the Middle Ages often discriminated among groups, but on the basis of culture or religion rather than "racial" attributes. Even in Spain and Portugal, racial difference began to define the status of slaves only at the end of the fifteenth century. It took yet a longer time before a fully developed racist ideology of subordination would come into being.

Cox argued that the socio-economic matrix of racial antagonism grew out of the commercialization of human labor in the New World. It resulted from intense competition among the leading nations for raw materials, markets, and cheap labor for the purpose of exploiting the natural resources of the New World. This, for Cox, was the beginning of modern race relations. They did not result from a "natural" feeling of antagonism based on the ostensible characteristics of ethnic difference or skin color. The development of a specifically racial ideology of subordination, white supremacy, served the practical purposes of justifying and facilitating the exploitation of labor:

> The capitalist exploitation of the colored worker, it should be observed, consigns them to employments and treatment that is humanly degrading. In order to justify this treatment the exploiters must argue that the workers are innately degraded and degenerate, consequently they naturally merit their condition (Cox 1970, 334).

The ideology of white supremacy was thus political and economic in origin and in no way depended on the actual experience of its proponents:

> The ultimate purpose of all theories of white superiority is not a demonstration that whites are in fact superior to all other human beings but rather to insist that whites must be supreme. It involves primarily a power rather than a social-status relationship. Assimilation diminishes the exploitative possibilities (Cox 1970, 335-336).

White supremacy served to make the exploitation of labor legitimate within specific historical circumstances. The sum of such an ideology was to reduce society to the status of nature by fixing and sustaining existing social relations. Cox claimed that such an ideology is invariably accompanied by force and extremes of violence, though he did not incorporate this into a theory of the state. He attempted to demonstrate only that there is a relationship between white supremacist ideology and violence that is part of a characteristic development of a racial division of labor in capitalist society. Racism is not, in this context, simply a system of beliefs but a relationship of power mediated by the ensemble of social institutions that make up the formal structure of society. He argued that although the manifest aspects of this division of labor have been historically transformed, particularly since the abolition of slavery, its fundamental imperatives continued to operate through the middle of the twentieth century. This should have led Cox to conclude that reforms in the area of race relations are likely to be more cosmetic than real. Indeed, his early work led him precisely to such a conclusion. But, as will be discussed below, he eventually opted for reformist strategies presumably based on a reconsideration of the historical conditions established in the aftermath of the civil rights movement of the 1960s.

Cox attempted to provide a plausible account of the origin and persistence of racism as an institutional practice in terms of the internal logic of an historically specific social system rather than simply as a narration of a linear development. Consequently, the continuation of racism in new forms is understood as grounded in capitalist social relations of production rather than in human nature or universal human experience. Racial segregation and discrimination appear, from this point of view, to be features of the dynamics of the capitalist economy and not as an aberration of an established moral order or the failure to achieve the full democracy presumably promised by the industrial revolution and ratified as such by the United States Constitution.

The legal system of segregation was still practiced in 1948 throughout the South and in parts of the northern United States. This system was the immediate focus of Cox's analysis, and he examined it in the context of the prevailing racial division of labor within the United States and world capitalism. Cox viewed segregation as a device for limiting the aspirations and prospects of black people as a group. It was a form of imprisonment for blacks which served to divide the working class along racial lines and, as a consequence, to weaken the social power of labor in general.

The primary aim of segregation was to establish and maintain the inferior position of blacks in society. The ideology of racism was reinforced by the use of legal and extra-legal violence to this end. Segregation was, for Cox, an inherently unstable social system in which the oppressed and exploited consistently refused to accept the inevitability of a situation that they nevertheless found difficult practically to oppose. Therefore, he argued, acts of individual and group rebellion were always a danger to the order of white supremacy. This danger could only be temporarily contained by mob terror and lynching, and the legal aspects of segregation were only able to forestall resistance, never to quell it altogether.

Cox argued that the system of racial segregation was undemocratic because it denied the full political rights of citizenship to black Americans and, as such, facilitated a regression within society by weakening the solidarity and social power of labor in its more comprehensive struggle for political and economic democracy. Under its influence, labor unions remained weak and ideologically conservative while neither a labor nor a socialist party was able to develop as a vehicle for political struggle.

Democracy and Class Struggle

Cox also wrote a series of essays in the 1940s which analyzed the relationships among capitalism, socialism, and democracy. Most of these appear in *Caste, Class and Race* in a section entitled "Class." They are uneven in quality and analytical sophistication. Some attempted to refine the theoretical conception of social class, while others commented on the contemporary political situation, including the rise of Fascism, the state of the labor movement, and the Roosevelt era of government. From an initial reading of these essays, their relationship to racism is not immediately evident. However, they give substance to Cox's account as reflections on context.

Cox began his analysis of democracy by situating it within the development of capitalism and by distinguishing it from liberalism. By the latter he meant a system of property and social relations defined by individual rights and the separation of government and economy. Liberalism conceived of society as composed of autonomous individuals. As a political doctrine, it accepts severe limitations on popular sovereignty and the exercise of control by society over government and economy. It presupposes the existence of natural laws and natural rights which provide a foundation for the normative order of society and the progress of civilization.

Cox thought of democracy as a modern phenomenon insofar as it is a social system. It differs significantly from the form of democracy which is associated with the Greek polis. Modern democracy did not grow out of or develop as a higher stage of ancient democracy. In Cox's view, modern democracy was a direct outcome of the rise of capitalism. As a system of government it was fashioned to facilitate the economic relations of capitalist society and to promote economic growth and capital accumulation.

Cox described the development of modern democratic society in terms of three distinct periods: (1) the elimination of the vestiges of the feudal regime; (2) the establishment of the liberal regime of bourgeois capitalism; and (3) the attack upon the hegemony of capitalist democracy by the proletariat (Cox 1970, 225). He dated the beginning of the third period at the middle of the nineteenth century.

His aim in this discussion was to clarify the meaning of democracy. Central to his argument was the distinction between political and economic democracy. Without denying the importance of the former, Cox argued that economic democracy presupposes social control over the means of the production and distribution of goods and services. In his view, democracy was defined by popular authority, concern for the well-being of the masses, and the denial of the freedom to accumulate great wealth at the expense of the rest of society. This is not possible in a society defined by capitalist social relations. As a consequence, at a certain stage in historical development, democratic forces find themselves in conflict with the interests of the capitalist ruling class:

> Democracy, then, was made possible of achievement by the bourgeoisie, but it cannot be achieved by the bourgeoisie. In fact, the bourgeoisie is unalterably opposed to democracy. The task of establishing a democracy necessarily devolves upon the proletariat, and its final accomplishment must inevitably mean its supercession of capitalism (Cox 1970, 225).

But this is more than a national struggle. It occurs on both the national and global levels. Cox viewed existing societies as more or less democratic rather than as either democratic or not. He denied that any existing society had attained full democracy. He believed, similarly, that socialism was, in principle, more democratic than capitalism, although he did not provide a concrete analysis of any socialist society.

As will be discussed below, Cox believed that the struggle against racism is an integral feature of the struggle for democracy. He viewed the struggle for civil rights as part of a class struggle against the exploitative nature of the racial division of labor within capitalist society, and concluded that civil rights could only be fully attained by means of an organized and protracted struggle to extend democracy and social equality in a socialist society.

Classes and Political Class Struggle

The concept of social class in the 1940s was, to say the least, confused. Liberal sociologists often begged the question of the relation of class to the capitalist division of labor or resolved it by denying the relation altogether. Cox intervened in this by distinguishing between social and political class formations. He argued that the concept of social class was adequate as a description of status positions within a capitalist society, but was not relevant to the analysis of the modern class struggle in its political dimension.

Cox's definition of "social class" was thus closer to Max Weber than to Karl Marx. He believed that the Marxist conception of class was misleading because it failed to discriminate between the social and political dimensions of class relations, and it used terms such as "class in itself" and "class for itself" that were too vague for an adequate socio-political understanding of class struggle. It is in regard to this sort of understanding that he formulated his conception of the political class as something loosely connected to the Marxian "class for itself" but with the concrete dimensionality of what sociologists call "organization." For Cox, political classes are defined by and organized for struggle. Their existence is found in all complex societies. The specific conflict between the bourgeoisie and the proletariat is then an historically concrete type of political class struggle, the product of modern capitalist society.

Cox treats existing social class relations as the objective condition for the development of a political class conflict. However, the membership of a political class is not identical with that of the social class it represents:

> Although the political class is ordinarily weighted with persons from a special sector of the social-status gradient, it may include persons from every position (Cox 1970, 154).

The fundamental tasks of a political class are, therefore, organizational and ideological: "...unlike the social class, the political class seeks to attract members to itself, and group solidarity is highly valued" (Cox 1970, 155). This implies something like a class-representative party with the special role of leading the struggle to reorganize the institutional order of society and to socialize the means of production and distribution. The means for waging this struggle are determined by the balance of power among competing political formations at any given time.

According to Cox, the political class is preoccupied with gaining or maintaining control over the state. Such a class may be comprised of many political factions, but it becomes conscious of itself as a unity through propaganda and agitation. The objective position of the class, and its interests, must be communicated to the various constituent subgroups by its leadership.

Objective conditions do not themselves create a political class struggle. The existence of antagonistic social classes is a necessary condition for the development of political class struggles. These tend to be local and specific; as such, they do not challenge the basic organization of society. For example, the labor movement constitutes a political class struggle only under revolutionary conditions. Similarly, Cox argued, while the civil rights movement in the United States might become part of a revolutionary social movement, it was not itself capable of forming a political class struggle without achieving some degree of unity between black and white workers. This position led Cox to reject black nationalism as a viable political strategy. But he believed that the demand for political and civil rights was fundamentally a radical one requiring for its fulfillment the joint efforts of civil rights organizations, labor unions, and Communist and Socialist parties. Cox pointed in particular to the CPUSA's racial policies as exemplary of this sort of effort.

The Civil Rights Movement
Caste, Class and Race does not offer an analysis of the modern civil rights movement, though its concluding pages discuss the prospects for the development of such a movement in the United States. Cox believed that its ultimate goal must be the complete social, political, and economic integration of black people in United States society. However, his analysis of the conditions of political class struggle led him to conclude that black peoples' struggles could only be part of a movement for genuine equality, and that leadership could only succeed if it represented progressive democratic movement toward a socialist society as a whole, ultimately a global movement since racism was, in the last analysis, the product of imperialism.

Cox argued in 1950 that leaders of the civil rights movement could be either black or white. The key attribute of leadership was its capacity to represent "the common cause":

> The common cause of Negroes in the United States is not fundamentally limited to Negroes. It is in fact an aspect of the wider phenomenon of political-class antagonism inseparably associated with capitalist culture. A principle involved in the process of democratic development is at the basis of the Negro's cause, and for this reason leadership among Negroes is likely to be as effectively white as black (Cox 1950b, 229).

He wrote four important articles in the 1950s (1950a, 1950b, 1951a, 1951b), that analyzed the development of the modern civil rights movement in terms of the progress of democracy in capitalist society. He began by defining the concept of civil rights in relation to political and economic democracy:

> Civil rights are the attributes of "citizens," and particularly of citizens of the modern states. But the concept of citizenship in the modern state has always been limited. It has been essentially a complex of duties, privileges, and rights associated with degrees of economic power; and economic power has been the independent variable. Consequently, in modern society, the struggle for civil rights has been primarily directed toward the limitation of economic power as the major force determining

the nature of citizenship. In its essence, the struggle for civil rights is a struggle for the redivision of societal power (Cox 1951a, 354-5).

The extension of civil rights was seen to be part of the extension of democracy against privately controlled economic power:

> In the modern state, then, the common people, white and black, have had to struggle constantly against a definable dominant class for increments of citizenship rights (Cox 1951a, 355).

Racial conflict in the United States is not between black and white people, but between the white ruling class and black people as a whole. Consistent with his position in *Caste, Class and Race,* Cox continued in these articles to minimize the significance of hostility against blacks by poor whites and to stress instead the ruling class aim of weakening the social power of the working class through the racial division of society in order to maintain a racial division of labor.

According to Cox, the extension of democracy in general and the modern civil rights movement in particular are intrinsically subversive to capitalism. The achievement of full civil rights for all citizens is an essential condition of democracy and, in turn, is possible only through a significant transfer of economic power to society. Thus, Cox's analysis of the prospects for social equality implies that the relationship between socialism and democracy is one of a necessary condition to a desired state of affairs; and for the condition to be fulfilled, the civil rights movement must become part of a more comprehensive political-class struggle. It is in this sense that political reactionaries have been correct in claiming that "Communism" is the driving force behind the civil rights movement; but only in this sense.

Cox distinguished among four types of leadership strategy in the history of the civil rights movement: collaboration, nationalism, protest, and proletarianism (Cox 1950a, 459).

> 1. Collaboration proposes to achieve civil rights through indirect, ingratiatory, suppliant tactics. Its program is essentially that designed for Negroes by the white ruling class; hence it expects civil rights to be granted beneficently as a reward for development of good behavior and trustworthiness among Negroes (Cox 1951a, 361).
>
> 2. Nationalism among Negroes in the United States is tentative; it can hardly ever hope to attain fulfillment. And yet, it has been continually

excited as a counter-action to the established nationalism among whites. It is anti-assimilationist, nativistic, and group conscious (Cox 1951a, 362).

3. The ideology of the protest programs is founded in social morality and ethics. Its strategic area of operation lies within the breach of democratic preachments and practices. It takes the great American creed that all men are created equal at face value; and it insists that the Thirteenth, Fourteenth, and Fifteenth amendments to the Federal Constitution mean exactly what they say. Although in achieving its ends it must inevitably entail a significant modification of the status quo, protest ideology never brings the social system itself into question (Cox 1951a, 360).

4. Proletarianism embodies the most far-reaching and fundamental approach to the conquest of civil rights. It believes and acts upon the assumption that the problem of achieving civil rights is a problem of a class of people which very largely includes Negroes (Cox 1951a, 363).

These types were exemplified for Cox respectively by Booker T. Washington, Marcus Garvey, Walter White, and Paul Robeson.

Cox emphatically rejected both collaboration and nationalism. In his view, the collaborationist leader could only restrict the aspirations of the black masses, thereby serving the interest of the ruling class. This was his interpretation of Booker T. Washington's main role as leader during the period of "overt racial segregation."

His opposition to nationalist leadership was based upon strategic as well as theoretical considerations. Since blacks made up only ten percent of the United States population, they could not by themselves bring about a general and permanent change in their social status. Black nationalism could only increase the isolation of blacks in a context that required just the reverse and disrupt the course of progress.

Cox supported both the protest strategy of the NAACP leadership and the interracial class alliance promoted by the United States Communist Party because he believed that the struggle for civil rights was fundamentally a class struggle. The success of such a movement for equality depended on legislative action, judicial reform, and mass protest, all of which required a broad basis of support. Although there were real conflicts between the protest and proletarian movements, both were important to the long-term struggle against racism.

By itself, the NAACP lacked a clear political and economic analysis. Its leaders, according to Cox, assumed that full integration was possible without disturbing the existing political and economic order of society. Such a strategy needed a more radical orientation if it was to have any chance of going beyond short-run and temporary gains. The Communists, on the other hand, believed that full integration could only occur when capitalism was replaced by socialism.

Cox supported "the popular front" strategy of the late 1930s, and considered the Left to be crucial to the furtherance of the civil rights struggle. By the late 1940s, the impact of the cold war on the civil rights movement was beginning to force a separation between protest and proletarianism. Walter White's public attacks on the influence of the Communists on the civil rights movement evoked precisely the sort of patriotism that Cox was convinced could only support the racial division of labor and hence continued inequality. As a result of such pressure, W.E.B. Du Bois was forced, in 1948, to resign from the NAACP because of his sympathies for the Left.

The impact of anti-communism on the civil rights movement was similar to its impact on the labor movement. The organized Left was effectively excluded from normal participation in both, while cold war liberalism became the ideological alternative to political reaction, and the Marxist analysis of the relation of race to class was consigned to the narrowest of margins of critical but "impractical" ideas. By the mid-1950s, the struggle for racial equality was understood by most activists and intellectuals as that between the forces of reform and reaction. It was not until the mid-1960s that Cox would observe the reemergence of radicalism within this insecure and divided movement.

From Civil Rights to Black Power

Cox worked on his study of the world capitalist system during the late 1950s and early 1960s (Cox, 1959, 1962, and 1964). It was not until the mid-1960s that he returned to the study of race relations and then under new circumstances and with a less radical vision. In 1965, he wrote an introduction to Nathan Hare's *The Black Anglo-Saxons* (Cox 1965). It was a task undertaken reluctantly since Cox disapproved of Hare's book, seeing it as an extension of Frazier's critical study of the black middle class, *Black Bourgeoisie*. He felt that both books erred in attacking the modest but, in his view, significant achievements of the black middle class. He also believed that such studies promoted black nationalism as an ideological solution to the continuing racial problems in the United States. The "radical" race theories of Hare and Frazier seemed to Cox to reject the very possibility of an assimilation of blacks into the larger society.

His study of the civil rights and black power movements was published in 1976, two years after his death. Although he claimed that *Race Relations: Elements and Social Dynamics* presented a general theory of race relations, it is better read as a conjunctural analysis of the struggle for racial equality during the 1960s. Cox was distressed, in 1966, by the turn in the civil rights movement away from non-violence, universalism, and middle-class leadership to the ideology of "black power." He objected to what he viewed as the disruptive anti-civil rights elements of the new militant leaders of CORE and SNCC, and to the influence of Malcolm X:

> We tend to forget that the power and universal appeal of the Negro protest activities of the early sixties emanated from its character of "passive resistance" (Cox 1976, 299).

Cox praised the southern civil rights movement for its accomplishments during the early 1960s and the policies of the Johnson administration on civil and voting rights. But he was unable to show how the tactics of non-violent civil disobedience could be used effectively in the North or how they might have an impact on the numerous forms of institutional racism grounded in capitalist social relations. Martin Luther King and the SCLC had failed in 1966 to bring about significant change in race relations in Chicago by the methods that had worked earlier in the deep South. Cox's belief, in the twilight of his career, in the future progress of race relations seems more to have expressed faith in the corporate liberal commitment to integration than to have been the result of the sort of careful political analysis for which his earlier work is known.

Cox sincerely believed that if blacks became politically isolated, they would never achieve equality and, in any case, would risk reactionary assault from the organized right. This led him to conclude that blacks as a group were ultimately dependent upon white support and even white leadership:

> In the United States, it seems clear, Negroes may participate to advantage in the larger movement for social change, but they cannot realistically hope to lead it (Cox, 1976, 301).

It was in this light that he became concerned with the role "lower class" blacks were playing in the black power movement and the influence of nationalist leaders on it, particularly Malcolm X, H. Rap Brown, and Huey Newton. If, as Cox had come to believe, middle-class culture had become the source of progressive universalism, then it must be the dominant force in any progressive movement for social change.

By the early 1970s, the theory of internal colonialism was used by Marxists as well as black nationalists to explain the political and economic situation of blacks in the United States. Cox was critical of this model, comparing it with the caste theory of race relations that he had criticized more than two decades earlier:

> Some years ago there was a popular school of race relations which defined blacks and whites in the United States as constituting two castes. The groups thus conceived were compared in detail and identified with relationships among Hindu castes. There is currently an opposite, rapidly developing tendency to regard American race relations as essentially a form of colonialism. Negroes, it is said, are colonials seeking "liberation" (Cox 1976, 274-5).

Each model used an analogy in place of an adequately theorized set of explanatory concepts. Each began by identifying features of racial discrimination that appeared in common with caste and colonialism and concluded that the appearance indicated an underlying identity which was itself neither substantiated empirically or conceptualized in its own right.

Cox did not deny that similarities existed. But the extension of the analogy was tantamount to denying the historical specificity of the situation of blacks in the United States. He believed that the theory of internal colonialism led to the political illusion that the strategy of national liberation was suitable in urban centers of the United States. In his view, these centers lacked the degree of political and economic autonomy that made it possible for anticolonial movements to succeed in other countries. For the United States, Cox argued in the 1970s, only non-violent protest could be the appropriate strategy for overcoming racial discrimination. His analysis of "the world system" led him to conclude that the structural contradictions of capitalism would lead to crisis in the Third World, not the United States, Western Europe, or Japan. In the near future, the most that could be hoped for in the advanced centers of capitalism were social democratic reforms of the existing system and it was to this possibility that, at the end of his life, Cox hoped to encourage activists to turn their attention.

Conclusion
One of the reasons it is difficult to evaluate the changes that took place in

Cox's views from the 1940s through the 1970s is that he provided little reflection on his own intellectual evolution. There are very few references throughout those four productive decades to how he developed the formulations presented in *Caste, Class and Race,* and how those formulations were reworked, transformed, or rejected by reference in later works to historical developments. As a result, the reader is left with a series of theoretical transitions and lost problems. The relationship between racism and class struggle and the contradictory character of capitalist democracy pass beyond the horizon between the early 1950s and the 1970s, along with the possibility that the struggle for socialism might solve the problems of racism and the dictatorship of the market. While it is easy enough to draw conclusions about these changes by referring to the events of the intervening decades, Cox provides few clues for readers interested in interpreting them as the result of the encounter of theoretical accomplishment with historical reality.

In part, the absence of reflection, a curious feature of Cox's work, may be traced to his positive, though not positivistic, conception of social science. Even though his research often led him to radical political conclusions, he nevertheless assumed that his work was primarily responsible to facts and only indirectly and abstractly influenced by political considerations as such. This led him to argue for institutions that provided value-neutral conditions for scientific research. He felt that Marx's own work had been compromised by his political activities in the labor and socialist movements of the nineteenth century.

Consistent with this view of science as essentially detached, and its theories essentially controlled by facts, Cox never joined any socialist or Communist organizations. Like Max Weber, with whom he seems to have agreed on the nature of social science, Cox believed that history could only be understood by means of a theory of social and economic development constantly modified by empirical research. This led him to pursue his historical research and it accounts for the movement of his thought through his trilogy on the world system. The exact course of that movement appears, due to Cox's lack of interest or belief in the value of metatheoretical reflection, to be more intuitive than an attempt to fully realize a theoretical project.

It is clear that crucial political and economic changes took place during the four decades in which Cox wrote, and that his way of understanding the relationship between capitalism and racism was in some ways fundamentally transformed by the encounter of concept with fact and experience. Cox was faced, fundamentally, with the fact that race relations were changed by the civil rights movement but that racism had not been abolished. Rather than being in decline, it has been integrated into the existing political economy in new ways. These changes might have accounted for Cox's revision of his initial theoretical proposals and his movement from a politics of revolution to one of reform.

Cox's study of the world system provided an understanding of the historical dimensions of capitalism on a global scale that was not congenial to revolutionary practice in the leader nations and was inimical to the prospects of a socialist movement led by the working class in the United States. He was led, in a period of intense anti-colonial struggles for national liberation, to the conclusion that the major crises within the world system were manifest in the periphery rather than in the leader nations.

These conclusions provided some of the background assumptions for what must appear to have been a retreat to conservatism in his later analyses of race and class relations. But if, as a result of social changes between World War II and the early 1970s, it was reasonable to see the United States as the leading nation of the world capitalist system, its society as open in new ways to liberalizing reforms within the framework of capitalist social relations, and the civil rights movement as having run its course, then one might well have concluded that an improved social position for black people was possible only through non-violence and reform. The initial alliance in practice between blacks and the United States working class had been transformed by events into an alliance in prospect between the civil rights movement and corporate liberalism. The historical dynamic of class struggle had been replaced by the intentions and possible accomplishments of the liberal reform movement of the late 1960s.

To some degree, the theoretical formulations of *Caste, Class and Race* contributed to Cox's critique of the nationalist aspirations of the black power movement. His response to the nationalist movement of the 1960s resembled in tone W. E. B. DuBois' and A. Philip Randolph's reaction to Marcus Garvey and the black nationalist movement of the 1920s. However, unlike DuBois or Randolph, Cox did not appreciate the positive role nationalism has played in the black struggle as well as in progressive coalition politics.

Similarly, Cox's belief in the importance of white leadership for the civil rights movement in the 1940s and 1960s may have led him, too easily, to rely on the middle class as his final designated representative of the prospect for democracy and racial equality. In the process, it appears that he ended by rejecting the very movement that he had devoted his life's work to sustaining in favor of a promise of reform that could only be fulfilled if the substance of his critique of capitalism and racism was incorrect from the beginning.

REFERENCES

Cox, Oliver C. 1950a. "The New Crisis in Leadership Among Negroes," *Journal of Negro Education* 19, Fall, 459-65.

_____. 1950b. "Leadership Among Negroes in the United States," in *Studies in Leadership*, ed. Alvin W. Gouldner. New York: Harper and Brothers.

_____. 1951a. "The Program of Negro Civil Rights Organizations," *Journal of Negro Education*, Summer, 1951, 354-66.

_____. 1951b."The Leadership of Booker T. Washington," *Social Forces*, 30, October, 1951, 91-97.

_____. 1959. *The Foundations of Capitalism*. New York: New American Library.

_____. 1962. *Capitalism and American Leadership*. New York: New American Library.

_____. 1964. *Capitalism as a System*. New York: Monthly Review Press.

_____. 1965. "Introduction," in *The Black Anglo-Saxons* by Nathan Hare. New York: Marzani and Munsell,

_____. 1970. *Caste, Class and Race*, New York: Monthly Review Press.

_____. 1976. *Race Relations: Elements and Social Dynamics.* Detroit: Wayne State University Press.

Index

About the Author

George Snedeker received his Ph. D. from the City University of New York in 1981. He teaches Sociology at the State University of New York/ College at Old Westbury and serves on the editorial board of the journal, *Socialism and Democracy*.